PRAISE FOR SONSHIP: RESTOF

"Jay's strong heart for God and others is clearly apparent in this devotional. His discerning insight fortifies these reflections to be provocative and challenging. These devotions pulled on my heart strings and convicted me to seek a deeper commitment to God's mission. I thoroughly enjoyed how I was stirred to look at life through a Kingdom-focused lens. This is a must read for every man!"

- Damon Hawkins
Area Director for Man in the Mirror

"Jay Cookingham's devotional book "Sonship," is a transformational book forged out of the fiery battles that Jay personally experienced, and the victorious kingdom lifestyle he stepped into as a son because of encountering Father God's extravagant love. In my opinion, Jay's book is not just a devotional book but a prophetic book that calls on men to contend for their identity, discover the secret of sonship and manifest their sonship. I highly recommend this book to any man who wants to live unashamedly as a true follower of Jesus Christ, especially in a world desperately in need of authentic men who are godly examples of Christ-likeness."

-Eric N. Supen
Author of several books including Kingdom Lifestyle, Kingdom-Driven Prayers-Prayer Works! Trainer and Life Coach, Germany, http://esupen.wix.com/kingdom-lifestlye

"There are any number of devotionals in print and I'm sure many of them are great. The reason I'm recommending this one is, not only for its wonderful encouragement and great insight, but because of the author. I have known Jay Cookingham for more than 40 years. He is a friend and a brother who has walked with me through ups and downs, tears and a lot of laughter. The words and insights in this devotional come from a man who has been an example and mentor to many. It's because of his heart, experiences and humility that the words bring life."

- Paul Grimsland
Program Director, Hope4Change-Philippines

"Sonship: Restoring a Man's Identity is a motivating daily devotional for those seeking a deeper walk with Jesus. Cookingham challenges men to drop the act and get honest with ourselves, family, friends, and community. This devotional is a call to repentance, prayer, and commitment to our position as sons of God. It's packed with servant leadership principles you can use in your role at work, as husband, father, or ministry leader. If you are looking for a devotional that will to refresh your relationship with Jesus, look no further."

Duane K. Brown
University Adjunct Professor

"Every male needs a male! This devotional book is impactful and intentional, to the end that we as males continue to grow as mature Christian men! I highly recommend this book and applaud this author, my friend Pastor Jay Cookingham!"

Pastor Edwrin Sutton
Husband, Pastor, Author of Purpose Unleashed

SONSHIP
RESTORING A MAN'S IDENTITY

JAY COOKINGHAM

Sonship:Restoring a Man's Identity

www.strategicfathering.com

StrategicFathering
MINISTRIES

*This book is dedicated to my bride Christine,
who has rescued my heart.*

TABLE OF CONTENTS

"Quote me as saying I was mis-quoted." - Groucho Marx

We refuse to wear masks and play games. We don't maneuver and manipulate behind the scenes. And we don't twist God's Word to suit ourselves. Rather, we keep everything we do and say out in the open, the whole truth on display, so that those who want to can see and judge for themselves in the presence of God.
2 Corinthians 4:2 MSG

INTRODUCTION

The fake disguise affectionately known as Groucho glasses are one of the most familiar silly faces known across the world. For decades this false glasses, nose and mustache combo have graced famous and ordinary faces alike. They're funny looking and provide a good-natured laugh or chuckle for most everyone. Still, I think they represent a deeper truth about humanity.

People seem gifted at wearing masks and using them to hide. The goal of a mask wearer can be to cover up the past, to mislead, or to please people. This cover up is detrimental to our freedom. Inside every human heart is a deep yearning to be known. We hunger for recognition, and for our story to mean something. We want someone to know who we are, to find us interesting. The problem with wearing masks is that they blur the line between the cover-up and discovery. Like seeing the Groucho mask on someone, we know something is off but we're unsure of what it might be.

The failure to fit in or belong to a group fuels shame, often encouraging men to hide behind masks of distrust, coolness, or remoteness. Further impacting this issue are the demands of the false

9

expectations of others. These expectations beg us to wear masks to avoid labels from family, friends, coworkers and the image they want us to project. Mask wearing is an exhausting cover up power trip. The power is our imagined control over what others see and the trip punishes us with loneliness.

The camouflage covers our true identity and keeps us from freedom

I have discovered that many men share this masquerade problem and embed themselves in an espionage mission. They have spent most of their lives covering up, disguising themselves in fear of being discovered. The fear comes from having a misunderstanding of their identity as men. I know this from experience.

My story of sonship started in a dark place of abuse and neglect. My dad's assault on my identity was vicious and left me searching for meaning. I chose the mask of a clown, masking my pain and anger with humor. For years my father's words, threats and beatings echoed in my spirit and the caustic abuse pushed me deeper behind the mask.

Growing up in an abusive home may not seem like the correct environment for me to discover freedom, but this is where my story began. Living through this dark period of my life helped me uncover the secret to sonship.

The secret was discovering who my real father was. It was the unearthing of the greatest treasure there is; a relationship with Father God. This discovery is the encounter that completely changes a man and enables him to feel free and alive.

When I met Jesus, my unmasking began. It involved forgiveness and rediscovering what it meant to be a man. Removing a mask is difficult and painful but freedom fills the wounds with grace. It's risky to reveal what's behind a mask, but it's riskier to stay behind one. There's pain involved in both decisions, but unmasking is a productive pain, leading to the abundant life Jesus promises. As you experience life beyond the mask, you hunger for more and the cost is nothing compared to the freedom gained.

Sonship retooling will remove the mask, empowering us to face the world as ourselves, unafraid and free. Unmasked men can see themselves as sons, accepting the fullness of Father's love and trusting His definition of their masculinity.

God's love and acceptance of us removes the mask

There is a call on your life—whether you are a Christ follower or not—soon you will face a choice. To follow Christ and embrace all He created for you to fulfill (your mission) or not. You may think about it, mull it over, ponder it, meditate on it, and even study it, but you will decide, either to accept or reject this invitation. This is the first call to us, the call of Salvation. From sin yes, but salvation is more of a call to become someone new. We are called to be His sons, free and unmasked to fulfill the destiny laid out for us. Salvation gives us legs for the journey; unmasking clears our sight to see the path ahead.

The struggles that confront my heart also strengthen my faith and leave me hungry for more of the heart of God. Settling for less never did that for a man. A son's heart must be free, uncaged and hungry for redemption. Liberty empowered by redemption speaks deep to my identity as His son and shakes the dust of the past from my soul. As the dust settles, my redeemed, rescued heart looks more like Jesus.

I pray these devotions mess with you, disturb your comfort zone and get under your skin; as they got under mine. I hope the next thirty days release fierceness in you to fight for your freedom. I pray for an unquenchable thirst for the living water that flows from the Father's heart.

For the King!

Jay Cookingham

"One life is all we have and we live it as we believe in living it. But to sacrifice what you are and to live without belief, that is a fate more terrible than dying." - Jeanne d'Arc

"But you are a chosen generation, a royal priesthood, a holy nation, His own special people, that you may proclaim the praises of Him who called you out of darkness into His marvelous light."
1 Peter 2:9-10

DAY 1 - LEGEND

In the movie, Lord of the Rings: The Return of the King is this wonderful scene between Elrond (the Elf king) and Aragorn, (the future king of Gondor). The armies of men are gathering at a camp, preparing for battle, not far from the city of Minas Tirith (the capital of Gondor) where the evil armies of Sauron are attacking.

In one scene, Aragon is troubled, restless, and unable to sleep soundly. A guard awakens him and takes him to King Theoden's tent where Elrond waits. The Elf king arrives with the news that his daughter, Arwen, (Aragon's love) is dying, her fate tied to the darkness that is now spreading because of Sauron. To add to the bad news is the revelation of additional armies joining the enemy's cause and Elrod proclaims.

"You ride to war but not to victory."

To Aragon, hope seems lost.

Elrond, however, has not come empty-handed. He gives Aragorn the re-forged sword Andúril, the weapon used by Aragorn's father to defeat Sauron in battle many years before.

According to legend, this sword will lead to his defeat again when the true king (Aragon) returns to the throne of Gondor. Elrond encourages Aragorn to take the sword and embrace his true lineage as king.

Elrond: *You're outnumbered, Aragorn. You need more men.*

Aragorn: *There are none.*

Elrond: *There are those who dwell in the mountain.*

Aragorn: *Murderers. Traitors. You would call upon them to fight? They believe in nothing. They answer to no one.*

Elrond: *They will answer to the king of Gondor! [Pulls out Anduril]*

Elrond: *Anduril, Flame of the West, forged from the shards of Narsil.*

Aragorn: *Sauron will not have forgotten the sword of Elendil. The blade that was broken shall return to Minas Tirith.*

Elrond: *The man who can wield the power of this sword can summon to him an army more deadly than any that walks this earth. Put aside the ranger. Become who you were born to be.*

That last line moves me every time I hear it. Aragorn seizes the role offered, a symbol of hope for Middle Earth, and leaves the shadows for good. He undertakes a dangerous mission that may kill him before he regains the throne. Yet, by accepting the sword Andúril, his focus is on rescuing a kingdom.

This is the life we're called to!

You are a legendary creation, made in the image of God, called to a life of following Jesus. Your life matters because God says it does. You are on a holy mission, a calling and an epic journey to rescue others. Your heart, forged in the fire of the Father's love, moves you to love like Him. He designed you to impact this world with the way you live. This is who you are, a man—God's son—a man after His own heart.

Take up the Sword of the Spirit, the Word of God and bring hope to a dying world. Put away the Ranger, the part of you that drifts from your destiny. Become a man who follows hard after his King.

14

"Put on salvation as your helmet, and take the sword of the Spirit, which is the word of God." Ephesians 6:17

A son is legendary!

Unmasking Questions:

Do you feel you have drifted from your destiny?

Are you embracing all God has called you to?

What hope can you bring to the world?

Unmasking Prayer:

Father, Give me the strength to move past my failures and move in the direction of your heart. Forgive my sin and the doubt it causes in my spirit, I choose to trust in you and you alone. Help me to walk by faith and not give into the fear that failure produces. I know that you are faithful and just and will forgive me. In Jesus name, Amen!

"We need to find God, and God cannot be found in noise and restlessness. God is the friend of silence. See how nature - trees, flowers, grass- grows in silence; see the stars, the moon and the sun, how they move in silence... We need silence to be able to touch souls."- Mother Teresa

"God did this so that they would seek him and perhaps reach out for him and find him, though he is not far from any one of us."
Acts 17:27

DAY 2 - NEED

During one of my quiet times with Father God I made this journal entry.

"Often, it is so much easier to do something for God than to just trust in God."

This statement stirred thoughts about my faith and why I follow Jesus. Walking with Jesus for 50 plus years, I recognize how to do the "Christian Thing". I know how to talk, how to behave and when to use appropriate religious buzz words. The problem is this form of religion is like dancing the hustle (excuse the disco reference) complete with strange dance moves. This funky spiritual dance moves with religious conviction (the famous list of do's and don'ts) but hinders relationship growth with the God I proclaim to love.

Our huffing and puffing to impress God, our scrambling for brown-ie points, our thrashing about trying to fix ourselves while hiding our pettiness and wallowing in guilt are nauseating to God and are a flat out denial of the gospel of grace. - Brennan Manning

In other words, my dance moves do not impress God.

My journey with God does not depend on my natural ability or what talents I bring to the table. It's not my strength of character, my experience obeying commandments or my (assumed) wonderful grip of the Scriptures that move God to act on my behalf. None of these traits or any other I have moves the heart of God to accept me as a son.

It is simply my need.

I need the Father to enter my life daily and teach me new dance moves, ones aligning my heart with His. The discipline of a son is birthed from acknowledging our need of Him. Father God designed this journey; He knows maturity, obedience and "right doing" come with discovering His heart.

My decision to answer the call of discovery imbeds me in a relationship that changes and deepens my need of Him. It's a call that can't be ignored; or easily pushed aside. Pursuing a deeper relationship with the Father is in us, He put it there. We can try to push it aside or ignore it, but the need, the longing to know and be known by God will never be silent in our souls. The hunger is that great.

But, what do I do about the list?

The Ten Commandments are the foundational list for the Christian man and obeying them is essential for our faith. The Sacraments, Baptism, Communion, are good life practices. They can be the bridge, the step, or the trigger that awakens us to our need for more of Him. But the truth is deeper than that. We must remember that just following rules, obeying commandments, and observing sacraments, are not guarantees of intimacy with the Father.

As I move away from a work list mentality, (and funny dance moves) I realize that I am here for a purpose higher than just behaving myself. I'm here to be His son, to enjoy a life getting to know my Father and the purpose He has for me.

Sons need their Father!

Unmasking Questions:

Do you feel you have to earn the Father's love?

How close do you feel to the Father?

Is it easier for you to do something for God rather than trust you belong to Him?

Unmasking Prayer:

Father, we declare our great need of You. We are hungry men. Men that need You. We need to be with You, live and love like You. We ask not to satisfy our hunger, but increase it. Let it burn down deep, changing our hearts, and freeing us to follow you with everything we have. Amen

"This is the power of sonship; men who give their heart to the Father become free! They are motivated by relationship not by reward. They will follow the Father to the ends of the earth and help others on the way." - Jay Cookingham

"O my son, give me your heart. May your eyes take delight in following my ways." Proverbs 23:26

DAY 3 - FOLLOW

Imagine you are at your place of work, at the office, construction site, wherever. One day this stranger shows up, he stops by your cubicle or the coffee shop. He appears to be just passing by but he stops and says… come, follow me.

What would you do? Would you question his sanity, his motives? Are you crazy? Follow you where? Why should I follow you?

In Matthew 4: 18-21 we read what the disciples did when Jesus dropped by their work site.

"While walking by the Sea of Galilee, he saw two brothers, Simon (who is called Peter) and Andrew his brother, casting a net into the sea, for they were fishermen. (19) And he said to them, "Follow me, and I will make you fishers of men." (20)Immediately they left their nets and followed him."

Immediately they followed him, without hesitation. No background check; no asking co-workers for their opinion; they dropped their nets and followed the Master. These men exchanged an occupation for a calling.

There was urgency in the steps of Jesus and a passionate hunger to fulfill Father God's mission for Him. His invitation to journey with Him doesn't work for hesitant individuals or the "let me sleep on it" crowd. Jesus is going somewhere, and He calls us to go with Him... now! As His followers, we need life in our steps, and passion in accepting the path He leads us on.

"You cannot follow God in neutral." Erwin McManus

Jesus applies no pressure, no arm twisting, no gimmicks, no hard sell, no fine print, no strings attached. Just... come follow me. To follow Jesus is relationally motivated, transforming us into active, engaged and determined agents of change. Becoming focused disciples, moving beyond ourselves and leaving behind the neutral, passive parts of our heart.

This is the sweet spot of life, following Him.

"Then Jesus said to His disciples, "If anyone wishes to come after Me, he must deny himself, and take up his cross and follow Me. 25 "For whoever wishes to save his life will lose it; but whoever loses his life for My sake will find it." Matthew 16:24-25

Sons follow the Messiah!

Unmasking Questions:

What are you willing to drop to follow Christ?

What are you willing to pick up to follow Christ?

What motivates your heart to follow Christ?

Unmasking Prayer:

Father God, I trust in your strong hand. I trust in the training of my hands and my heart. Strengthen my resolve, my faith and vision. I rely on your full armor and every promise from your Word. I follow hard after your heart; I am driven by your spirit to your side. I will bow to no other King but You... my God and my deliverer! Amen!

"The God of light insists on traveling into dark places; the God of peace continuously involves Himself in the wars of men; the God who is good engages the depth of human evil. To follow Jesus is to enter the unknown, to relinquish security, and to exchange certainty for confidence in Him." - Erwin McManus

"The Lord is my light and my salvation; whom shall I fear? The Lord is the strength of my life; of whom shall I be afraid? Psalm 27:1

DAY 4 - MISSION

The Green Berets are some of the toughest men on the planet; they are the "special" of special ops. Their training, their dedication, and their sacrifice are off the charts.

Green Berets have five primary missions:

- Unconventional warfare (guerrilla warfare to overthrow an occupying power)
- Foreign internal defense (training allies how to fight)
- Special reconnaissance (behind enemy lines)
- Direct action (Taking the fight to the enemy, on their turf)
- Counter-terrorism. (attacking terrorist threats before they strike)

The Green Berets' motto got me thinking about freedom. Their motto is something special.

De Oppresso Liber — To Liberate the Oppressed

In the battle for the human heart, God did something wild and unconventional. He sent Jesus to liberate the oppressed, including you and me. He put a brilliant battle plan in motion, a countermeasure to the forces out to destroy the human heart and soul. Jesus went behind enemy lines, took the fight to the enemy and totally won the victory for us.

In Romans 5: 7-8 we read His battle plan.

"God demonstrated his own love for us, in that while we were still sinners, Christ died for us"

We are the liberated; the set free ones, now we get to fight for the freedom of others. Our mission is special because redemption not only invites us into the Father's heart; it also invites us into His work. In Luke 4:18, Jesus lays out the mission plan.

"The Spirit of the LORD is upon me, for he has anointed me to bring Good News to the poor. He has sent me to proclaim that captives will be released, that the blind will see, that the oppressed will be set free."

Jesus charged into life with the purpose of setting people free, going wherever they happened to be. In modern day context that could be bars, clubs, strip joints, bingo halls, or city hall. Speculation of Jesus' mission strategy is great to debate and muse about but I'm sure we would all be surprised where He would turn up.

However, Jesus does "turn up" where we go, the places we frequent, visit and live by. We are called to share the message of the Gospel to a dark world every day. Father God sends us into the risky and heroic action of touching the lives of other human beings to reach the world He loves. It takes faith to walk out this plan and calls for a heart of obedience. When we surrender all to the Father's way—like Jesus did—there is no surrender to any other force. This is the way to liberate the oppressed, by following His heart.

Sons go on mission!

Unmasking Questions:

What have you been liberated from?

Are you afraid of following Christ to dark places?

What do you think your mission is?

Unmasking Prayer:

"Take, O Lord, and receive my entire liberty, my memory, my understanding and my whole will. All that I am and all that I possess You have given me. I surrender it all to You to be disposed of according to Your will. Give me only your love and your grace; with these I will be rich enough, and will desire nothing more."
- St. Ignatius - 16th century

"True nobility is exempt from fear." - Shakespeare
(King Henry the Sixth, Part II Act IV, Scene I)

"But the noble man makes noble plans, and by noble
deeds he stands." Isaiah 32:8

DAY 5 - NOBLE

In the movie Braveheart, William Wallace becomes a central figure in the revolt to secure Scottish freedom from the English. Following the exploits of Wallace is Robert the Bruce, the leader of the Scottish Noblemen. He is a man in conflict, feeling the tug of joining the fight or staying the course of entitlement. His father (dying of leprosy) keeps whispering in his ear to bide his time, to wait for the right time to "rise up" but in reality is keeping his son from becoming a great leader.

This movie makes me think how much passivity makes us act like Robert the Bruce. A leader inspires us and boldly we run off to join his cause. Then we are reminded of our holdings, the land and comfort we own. We buy the lie that the enemy is too strong to conquer, and it's not the right time for such boldness. We think that if we're patient, if we bide our time, then we can overthrow the enemy in our lives. The truth is that the waiting, the laying back, lulls us to inactivity and eventually spiritual slaughter. All we thought we possessed has seductively fallen into enemy hands. We don't realize how "occupied" we have become. It is worse than the disease that was wasting his father's flesh; it's the decay of true nobleness.

The possibility of having their own freedom didn't motivate the "nobles". It meant risking the loss of what they already had. Contrast that to this Scripture in the book of Isaiah:

"But the noble thinks noble things; and by noble things he shall stand." Isaiah 32:8

A noble heart is bold and ready to act; it doesn't give way to passivity. This heart does not back down from fear, it rises up and stands for what is right. Nobleness frees a man's heart to follow a heart greater than his own. This heart grows bigger when it runs on a trail of obedience.

"I will run in the way of your commandments when you enlarge my heart!" Psalm 119:32

On this path sons learn the faithfulness of obedience, super-sizing their hearts as they run in the Father's way. Becoming agents of hope, marking the trail for others to follow, challenging them to leave the orphan life behind and live as sons. We deliver hope by courageously coming alongside someone when they're in need. By allowing someone's voice to be heard when no one wants to listen. Noble men clear the trail of despair by believing in someone when no one else will, everything the Father's does for us!

Nobility is a relational marker of who we are in Christ but it is also an action. Our No-bility, is the power to say no to lesser things and yes to Kingdom things. That's the inner strength needed in the daily fight for our hearts. We need to be noble men, if there is a war for our hearts; our loved one's hearts are also on the hit list. Noble sons fight for God's kingdom and the hearts of the people He loves.

Sons are noble men!

Unmasking Questions:

How's your No-bility today, what are you saying no to?

Are you too comfortable?

Who can you mark the trail for today?

Unmasking Prayer:

Father, Move me in such a way that I become courageous to fight and to care in ways I didn't think possible of me. Help me to be a noble man, standing for what is right. Awaken the spiritual warrior in me to do battle as you see fit, for your glory and for the freedom of many. In Jesus name we pray. Amen

"America must win this war. Therefore, I will work, I will save, I will sacrifice, I will endure, I will fight cheerfully and do my utmost, as if the issue of the whole struggle depended on me alone." - Diary of Martin Treptow – WW1 solider killed in action

"More than that, we rejoice in our sufferings, knowing that suffering produces endurance, and endurance produces character, and character produces hope." Romans 5:3-4

DAY 6 - ENDURE

In 1958, William Sangster, the great Methodist Preacher, speaking in Texas started having difficulty swallowing and walking. Shortly afterwards, he was diagnosed with progressive muscular atrophy, an incurable neurological disease. Undaunted, he made four life affirming resolutions and kept them throughout his remaining years: They were: 1) I will never complain; 2) I will keep the home bright; 3) I will count my blessings; 4) I will try to turn it to gain. To this list he added daily intense prayers. One of his prayers was a battle cry, revealing the heart of an unbowed warrior.

"Let me stay in the struggle, Lord", he pleaded. "I don't mind if I can no longer be a general, but just give me a regiment to lead".

Endurance is extreme resilience in the face of intense struggle. The courage it takes to suffer physical, emotional, relational pain and go on strong is amazing and that courage describes the heart of our Lord Jesus.

"So then, since Christ suffered physical pain, you must arm your-selves with the same attitude he had, and be ready to suffer, too. For if you have suffered physically for Christ, you have finished with sin. (2) You won't spend the rest of your lives chasing your own desires, but you will be anxious to do the will of God." 1 Peter 4:1-2

Peter is urging us to endure hardship as Jesus did; humble, focused and faithful to His Father's will. Christ's approach towards suffering teaches us a powerful truth of why our lives matter. Life isn't a series of random, unrelated events without purpose; they connect us to the larger story of Redemption. Endurance is spiritual grit; preparing us for action in the war for freedom. Warriors accept that there will be hardship in a battle that sets people free.

We are to arm ourselves with the same powerful stance of Christ, adopting His attitude of doing whatever is necessary to complete the mission, no matter the cost. This determination frees our heart to see purpose in our suffering, and that is a huge weapon against despair.

Adversity pours out poison to rob hope from a warrior's heart, and suffering can beat a man's spirit to death. Thankfully, to "endure" does not mean to suffer without reason. Enduring is focused faith in the goodness of God and trusting in His plan. The Father's objective is our freedom, thus making us more dangerous (to the enemy) than what we thought we could be.

"As it is written: "For Your sake we face death all day long; we are considered as sheep to be slaughtered." (37) No, in all these things we are more than conquerors through Him who loved us." Romans 8:36-37

According to this Scripture we are not just conquerors, but super-conquerors primed for victory. The question for a warrior son is how we define victory in the face of suffering. Is it rescue from hard times without suffering or something deeper that defines a conqueror? The cross of Jesus and His resurrection from the dead is the compelling answer to this soul search. Messiah's suffering and sacrifice produced a decisive victory, overcoming sin, death and the destruction they cause. The lesson is clear; a warrior learns that victory is defined by freedom gained, not by the lack of suffering.

32

Sons, despite the opposition, embrace the struggle and stay faithful to the mission. We persevere, we fight on, and we endure hardship because love fuels a Kingdom warrior's heart. A fierce and pure love for his God and the people entrusted to his care.

Sons endure the battle for the Kingdom of Christ!

Unmasking Questions:

What is the worst hardship you've ever experienced?

Have you ever had to endure physical or emotional pain because of your faith in Christ?

Have you ever felt the pain you went through was worth it?

Unmasking Prayer:

Father, I have need of endurance; I grow weary too easily when my heart is far from You. My soul declares that You are my strength and I depend only on You. Give me the mind of Christ and His passion to follow your will with all the strength I have.
In Jesus name, Amen

"I know what I'm capable of; I am a soldier now, a warrior. I am someone to fear, not hunt." - Pittacus Lore, The Rise of Nine

*"What good is it, dear brothers and sisters, if you say you have faith but don't show it by your actions?
Can that kind of faith save anyone?" James 2:14*

DAY 7 - UPROAR

Somewhere out of the deepest part of my spirit a question often surfaces with a familiar sting to it. Provoked by the great disturber of my complacency, the Holy Spirit, the sacred inquiry rises and challenges my faith to action. The question is a strange and powerful one.

Are you looking for trouble?

Labeled a blasphemous troublemaker by the Jewish religious leadership of His day, Jesus is busy causing trouble. Healings, preaching the Good News and proclaiming the arrival of a new kingdom has branded Jesus an enemy of the State. His ruckus has His followers uneasy and afraid for their own lives.

The night before the cross, those followers, His closest friends, betray Him and run away, leaving Jesus to face His accusers alone. Tried, convicted and executed by the Roman government on a cross meant for criminals. The Romans were good at suppressing rebellion, using the cruelty of the cross to punish and discourage troublemakers. Yet, Jesus takes this violent symbol of death and connects the cross with His uproarious mission to bring new life into the world. Now, thousands of years later, Jesus is still inviting followers into the fray.

"If anyone would come after me, let him deny himself and take up his cross and follow me. Matthew 16:24

Jesus holds up the cross as the desired route for causing uproar in the world. This path of self-denying, sacrificial love challenges the human heart to follow His lead. He created uproar after uproar by loving people out of darkness and into the light. His love penetrated racial barriers and gender barriers, challenging the religious community's inability to love one's neighbor as oneself.

To cause such a spiritual riot is to be labeled a troublemaker by a world needing Gospel upheaval in their souls. Kingdoms of hatred, racism and injustice need overthrowing, but they will fight back ferociously and not let go of their captives easily. The uproar begins with embracing a life of disruptive humility. Nothing fuels an uproarious lifestyle like loving people the way they need to be loved. That takes a man walking closely with His God.

"He has told you, O man, what is good; and what does the LORD require of you but to do justice, and to love kindness, and to walk humbly with your God?" Micah 6:8

The love of Christ is not timid, tame or domesticated; it's a robust, fierce response to evil, never yielding to passivity. His love does not sacrifice itself on the altar of public opinion or hide from the commotion it creates. Instead, it confronts indifference with passionate resolve and purpose, leaving apathy in the dust.

The resulting turbulence may be a bumpy ride, but to move, stir, and shake loose captive hearts requires a heart full of uproarious love. The wake we leave upsets the plans of the enemy because our obedience signals our intent to follow hard after Christ. This message leaves no room to doubt who we serve and who we trust.

"Many are the troubles of a righteous man but God delivers him from them all" Psalm 34:19

I see that passage as a battle cry to my masculinity and my faith. The imagery of wild and threatening events urges my heart to be battle ready. My faith causes uproar in the enemy camp; it disturbs the forces of darkness. A son's obedience to the Father always does.

Sons lives uproariously!

Unmasking Questions:

When was the last time you caused a ruckus?

Where have you settled for words without actions in your faith?

How can you become more involved in the uproarious way of Jesus?

Unmasking Prayer:

"Disturb us, Lord, when we are too well pleased with ourselves, when our dreams have come true because we have dreamed too little, when we arrive safely because we have sailed too close to the shore.

Disturb us, Lord, when with the abundance of things we possess, we have lost our thirst for the waters of life; having fallen in love with life, we have ceased to dream of eternity; and in our efforts to build a new Earth, we have allowed our vision of the new heaven to dim.

Disturb us, Lord, to dare more boldly, to venture on wider seas where storms will show your mastery; where losing sight of land, we shall find the stars. We ask you to push back the horizons of our hopes; and to push into the future in strength, courage, hope, and love."

- Sir Francis Drake

"There are far, far better things ahead than any we leave behind."
- C.S. Lewis

"I have told you all this so that you may have peace in me. Here on earth you will have many trials and sorrows. But take heart, because I have overcome the world." John 16:33

DAY 8 - BATTLE

The walk around my neighborhood was filled with prayers; I felt an anointing and power in the words I spoke over my city. As I walked into a dark section of my neighborhood, I came up against an even darker force threatening me. I remember the threat vividly. It was clear, direct, and the words were filled with hatred.

"I'm going to kill you," the voice said.

I at once rebuked the enemy with all the authority that was given me as a son of God, but I took the threat seriously. Never be surprised by the pushback and the viciousness of the attack by this deceitful foe.

"Be sober-minded; be watchful. Your adversary the devil prowls around like a roaring lion, seeking someone to devour." 1 Peter 5:8

The battle for a man's heart is real and intensely fierce. Our opponent is focused and dead set against men living for God. This adversary is unashamed about wreaking havoc in our lives and destroying anything precious to the Father. He lies; he steals, he wants you dead, if not physically, then dead to the promises and purposes of God in your life.

He wants to rid the world of you.

This roaring lion loves to use our past against us and this becomes one of the toughest battles a man faces. We often allow past events, our mistakes, failures, and sins to haunt us into accepting something less than God's best. The barriers of our regrets fight against us, telling us that we're not good enough, that we don't have what it takes or that we are damaged goods. We lose focus, our identity becomes blurred (or worse) and we fall back into the shadows of passivity. This is deadly for a man's heart and his walk with God.

How do we respond?

The enemy wants to defeat our heart, make it hard and unresponsive to the Father. So we could get hardheaded, hard-nosed, hard as nails, hard to the core. We could shrink back, lose heart, choose a different way or we can choose to have the Father's heart pressed into ours. For whatever or whoever has your heart... has you.

"And I will give you a new heart, and I will put a new spirit in you. I will take out your stony, stubborn heart and give you a tender, responsive heart." Ezekiel 36:26

What we believe about our hearts matters. If it's valuable (God thinks so) we'll protect it, fight for it and worship the God who created it! The enemy wants us to believe our heart doesn't matter to the Father, that it's unredeemable, corrupt and beyond hope. Thankfully, the truth is miraculously more powerful, Father God restores our hearts with His.

"I will give them a heart to know me, for I am the LORD; and they will be my people, and I will be their God, for they will return to me with their whole heart."Jeremiah 24:7

The battle for a new heart is more than a transplant of values; it is a radical new way to live. It's a heart that beats with a rhythm of relationship with the Father, responding in the only way that brings life. This is huge, for us to move through a hard life without growing hard and cold, we need His Spirit breathing new life into our hearts.

Sons battle for their heart!

Unmasking Questions:

What is your toughest battle?

How are you engaging in this fight, how are you taking it to the enemy?

What area in your life do you need courage/boldness/strength?

Unmasking Prayer:

Heavenly Father, We are your sons, we will not back down, we will not quit and we will not give our hearts to lesser things. Our hearts are yours; our strength is yours, our minds, our spirits and all we are as men belong to you. Infuse us with humility, empower us with boldness and fill us with your love. Let honor, nobility, and integrity join our hearts together as one. I pray that our lives will be powerful expressions of worship and service to You. In the mighty name of Jesus I pray, amen!

"Repentance, not proper behavior or even holiness, is the doorway to grace. And the opposite of sin is grace, not virtue."
- Philip Yancey

"I have swept away your sins like a cloud. I have scattered your offenses like the morning mist. Oh, return to me, for I have paid the price to set you free." Isaiah 44:22

DAY 9 - TURN

Our soul lives in a war zone. This world wounds us daily with a bombardment of selfish pursuits wooing us away from God's heart. Every engagement between us and this world seeks to drive a wedge between us and the life that would free us. Sin is a poison, clouding the minds of humanity and causing great destruction throughout our world. Sin steals our heart away from God.

Why do we believe the lies and allow the theft of our heart? When did sin management become the replacement for repentance? What has led us to believe we can sin as we please because we "know" God will forgive us? Could it be that in our desire to be happy we have lost our longing to be Holy?

There is a way to turn us around.

"From that time Jesus began to preach, saying, "Repent, for the kingdom of heaven is at hand." Matthew 4:17

Jesus knew that to change a heart's direction you need radical repentance. The word radical means to use extreme measures to change something. In the medical world, radical surgery is designed to remove the root of a disease or diseased tissue in someone. Sin is the root of spiritual disease in the human mind, heart and soul, it needs to be removed. Radical repentance is the surgery we need and the spiritual surgical procedure is powered by the Father's kindness.

"Or do you despise the riches of His kindness and forbearance and patience, not knowing that the kindness of God leads you to repentance?" Romans 2:4

Did you get that? God leads us to repentance, He shepherds us back into repentance. Not a big stick, no threats, just a heart that yearns to be reconnected with His creation. Sin wants you to remember your failure, the wrong you have done, but repentance remembers the goodness of the Father and returns to Him.

Acts 3:19 (Greek meaning in parentheses)

"So repent (change your mind and purpose); turn around and return to God, that your sins may be erased (blotted out, wiped clean), that times of refreshing (of recovering from the effects of heat, recovery of breath) may come from the presence (the face) of the Lord."

Repentance clears the slate, removes the evidence, giving the enemy no ammunition to use against us. This heart/mind/soul change is not behavior modification or sin management; but rather declaring war on sin. Repentance is yielding and stepping into real life transformation!

2 Corinthians 7:10 (Greek meaning in parentheses)

"For godly grief (sorrow) produces a repentance (reversal, reformation) that leads to salvation without regret, whereas worldly grief produces death."

This is a deep inner man change; a decision birthed from Godly sorrow, a reversal from what we once thought acceptable. Godly sorrow is not what convinces God to forgive us, the blood of Jesus does that, but this sorrow breaks down mental strongholds that keep us from freedom. This mental transformation is more than just changing our minds, more than feeling bad for what we have done. This is a radical and deliberate transformation choice, helping us to walk as sons.

Repentance is a deep breath for the soul, it's a cleansing breath. It fuels the turning process our heart must respond to, leading us away from sin and back to the Father. This is the evidence of radical repentance, a fierce mindset that focuses on getting back into a right relationship with the Father. Radical repentance is a force the enemy can't stop.

Sons turn their heart, their soul, their mind back towards the Father!

Unmasking Questions:

Do you have difficulty repenting?

Have you ever been motivated to repent by "Godly Sorrow"? When?

What would radical repentance look like in your life if consistently practiced?

Unmasking Prayer:

Father, I confess my sin and repent from thoughts and actions that do not honor your name. Cleanse me from my wrongdoing, create a new heart in me, and restore a right spirit so that I might choose your ways over my own. I am sorry for my sin and now choose to set my face towards You. Help me to accept forgiveness and move forward with You. - Amen

"A life spent making mistakes is not only more honorable, but more useful than a life spent doing nothing." - George Bernard Shaw

"Jeremiah, say to the people, 'This is what the LORD says: "'When people fall down, don't they get up again? When they discover they're on the wrong road, don't they turn back?"
Jeremiah 8:4

DAY 10 - FAIL

I have failed in life at an epic level.

There were times I choked under pressure and bailed big time when situations were tough. There were too many days when my heart hid when it was needed most and I chickened out from caring. Because of selfish thoughts I covered my eyes, closed my ears and pretended not to notice suffering.

And those were my good days.

I sought success over significance, hungered ravenously for comfort over compassion and pleasure over purity. I frustrated my own dreams by fearing the outcome and dreading the journey. Escape was the path I desired, portrayals and roles were my game pieces, but I feared the hand I was dealt. I rolled the dice, taking a chance of discovery, but quickly folded under the pressure, so afraid of being found out, revealed and exposed as a fraud.

The Apostle Paul once commented, "I am the chief of all sinners." I think to myself... "He's never met me."

Here's my heart in this. Although I really don't think that my past failures make me a "dirty rotten sinner" anymore, I do realize how lost I am without Christ. It is this realization that fuels my hope. My heart was designed to be filled with Jesus, no matter how many times I've failed.

"I am not concerned that you have fallen... I am concerned that you arise." - Abraham Lincoln

Abe's quote here mirrors the Father's heart, in Psalm 37:23

"If the Lord delights in a man's way, he makes his steps firm; though he stumble, he will not fall, for the Lord upholds him with his hand."

Even while reading this Scripture I find my heart fearing the potential failure that follows falling. This fear lies to me, tugs on my sleeve, and fabricates a story of doubt and guilt. A story meant to immobilize my heart and stop me in my tracks, afraid to move out in faith. This enemy wants my heart to believe that I'm doomed to fail and that my failures are always fatal and final. I know the voice of failure; it's not a very kind one, but God's voice is different. His words carry a hopeful and distinct purpose, the Father's voice comes to rescue me.

"My health may fail, and my spirit may grow weak, but God remains the strength of my heart; he is mine forever." Psalm 73:26

"The godly may trip seven times, but they will get up again. But one disaster is enough to overthrow the wicked." Proverbs 24:16

"So do not fear, for I am with you; do not be dismayed, for I am your God. I will strengthen you and help you; I will uphold you with my righteous right hand." Isaiah 41:10

Father God picks us up and holds us in an upright position. His strength, His help sets us free and when we are set free from fear of failure, we are finally free to live.

Failures will try to rob us of identity and purpose, but sons are never failures in our Father's eyes. We may struggle, fail and fall down but none of those things define us, unless we allow them to. The Father will not let any failure define His sons. Only His Word and His purposes define who we are.

Sons are not failures!

Unmasking Questions:

Are you afraid of failing?

What was your biggest mistake and what did you learn from it?

If we learn from our mistakes, why are we always so afraid to admit them?

Unmasking Prayer:

Father, hear my prayer! I'm lost without You. My heart wants to give up without You. Without you my spirit longs to run away and hide. The strength I possess seems small without you. Without your presence, vision is dim and my way is too dark to see.

Where can a man like me go but to You, oh giver of life? With You my strength returns and my spirit finds the strength to go on. Vision returns when my eyes set on You alone. I can rejoice because I am exposed to the fullness of your love. I am set free in your presence... I am set free in your presence...
I am set free in your presence!

No good thing will you keep from me...your Word is good, your heart is good, your way is good and they will not be kept from me.

My declaration is this...I am yours because you made sure I was yours. Thank You for your sacrifice and the price you paid for me! In You alone will I trust! Amen!

"One person with passion is better than forty people merely interested."- E. M. Forster

"The LORD goes out like a mighty man, like a man of war he stirs up his zeal; he cries out, he shouts aloud, he shows himself mighty against his foes." Isaiah 42:13

DAY 11 - BURN

When firefighters describe a house fire that is totally involved, it means that the all the major rooms of the structure are on fire. In other words, the blaze is consuming every area of the structure; nothing is untouched by the inferno.

"Since we are receiving a Kingdom that is unshakable, let us be thankful and please God by worshiping him with holy fear and awe. (29) For our God is a consuming fire." Hebrews 12:28-29

God is a consuming fire, a fire that utterly consumes anything unholy because He is holy. This holiness demonstrates zealous love towards a world lost in sin and darkness. The Father's divine fire storm is redemptive, seeking to involve every chamber of the human heart, and every part of the human soul in the cleansing process. This refinement of love produces sons and daughters, former spiritual orphans now set free. The proper response of a free heart is worship, now on fire with a longing to serve the Father. Worship consumes us, creating a living sacrifice with an ongoing commitment to a loving relationship with a Holy God.

Of course opposition to such a powerful partnership is passionate as well. The enemy of our soul obsesses with creating havoc in our world. He confuses our identity with lies, stealing hope with disease and sorrow. His cruel and sickest wish is destroying what is precious to God, namely you and me. This adversary will suck the passion from us, neutralizing our heart and taming the mighty man inside us. That domestication comes with a cost to our manhood, causing us to settle for a less troublesome adversary.

"Many of us are hunting mice while lions devour the land."
- Leonard Ravenhill

There are seasons when the idols of comfort, pleasure, and safety, lull me to indifference. I confess the weakness of my heart for those moments when the fear of the hunt drives me into the shadows of apathy. I hate settling for less than God's best and what that surrender does to my heart.

The Greek word for zeal means "to boil". What better to have boiling inside then a faithful love for my King? So, I pray for the Holy Spirit to make my blood boil, to help me burn as I follow Jesus with everything I am. There are fierce lions devouring the land and I'm tired of hunting mice, I'm going after the big game. I hunger and burn to be like these heroes in Hebrews.

"By faith these people overthrew kingdoms, ruled with justice, and received what God had promised them. They shut the mouths of lions, quenched the flames of fire, and escaped death by the edge of the sword. Their weakness was turned to strength. They became strong in battle and put whole armies to flight." Hebrews 11:33-34

This passion fueled faith, connects us in a covenant relationship with a Holy God. We engage the lions head on, trusting God to turn our weakness into power and strength. We fight fire with Holy fire and every step of faith burns the imprint of our Father into us; releasing the mighty warriors inside us.

Sons are on fire!

Unmasking Questions:

What are you passionate about (or zealous for)?

Are you desperate/hungry/burning to live free?

What is the enemy using to attack your zeal?

Unmasking Prayer:

Father, may our zeal for you never fade! We pray that the burning desire to follow hard after you never grows cold. Stoke the passion for your presence, blow upon the flames of our heart so that we are consumed by your love. Let the motivation of our hearts be that we are a people called by your name, ready to obey and move in your purposes for your glory. Amen

"The battleline between good and evil runs through the heart of every man." - Aleksandr Solzhenitsyn

"Put on all of God's armor so that you will be able to stand firm against all strategies of the devil." Ephesians 6:11

DAY 12 - TARGET

In a key battle during the Korean War, Colonel Chesty Puller and his fellow Marines became surrounded by 7 enemy divisions (around 80,000 men) in a remote part of North Korea known as the Chosin Reservoir. Colonel Puller, one of the most decorated US Marines in history, responded this way:

"All right, they're on our left, they're on our right, they're in front of us, they're behind us...they can't get away this time"

This seasoned leader saw hope for victory despite the overwhelming odds. To him, being surrounded by the enemy was a favorable strategic position, not a situation to fear. Puller understood that an exposed enemy was easier to engage than one hiding in the shadows. His message to his men was clear, stop being a target, move forward and attack.

When we surrendered to Christ, we became a target to take out. We face an enemy desperate to surround us and cut us off from the Father. There is a price on our head; a hit list with our name on it and the devil intends to collect the bounty. Using the formidable weapon of deception, this cruel foe wages a brutal and lie infested propaganda war against us. His strategy of misinformation focuses on increasing fear, destroying hope and crushing our hearts.

Fear leads us to question what we know is the truth, leaving us in a dangerous position on the battlefield. This spirit of second guessing and denial helps the enemy zero in on our position. Passive targets are easier to hit and defeat, this the enemy counts on.

Yes, stepping out of darkness into the light left us vulnerable but not defenseless. In Christ we are dangerous to the enemy's plans and deception. Obedient sons walk in God's truth and stay engaged in the struggle for freedom. With so much at stake we no longer worry for our comfort or security but we fight to remove the target from others. God, our divine hero, trains and empowers us for the conflict we face.

"He trains my hands for battle; my arms can bend a bow of bronze." Psalm 18:34

Life behind enemy lines is never safe, but sons engage the enemy wherever the Master leads, and He will lead us into dark territory. Our adversary the devil rules the dark places, the shadows, with a cruel hand and does his greatest damage there. Shadow wars aren't minor skirmishes too distant to be a threat; the front lines are closer than we think. If you don't find the battle, it will find you. Let's remove the target and put on armor.

"You have armed me with strength for the battle; you have subdued my enemies under my feet." Psalm 18:39

In Ephesians 6:17, the Apostle Paul calls the Bible "the sword of the Spirit", it is a spiritual sword that cuts through lies and propaganda. The enemy of our soul fears this weapon because he knows God's Word is alive, powerful and exposes everything in its light.

"For the word of God is alive and powerful. It is sharper than the sharpest two-edged sword, cutting between soul and spirit, between joint and marrow. It exposes our innermost thoughts and desires. (13) Nothing in all creation is hidden from God. Everything is naked and exposed before his eyes, and he is the one to whom we are accountable." Hebrews 4:12-13

The Gospel message is decisive, giving us the edge in the war for freedom. The Father's Word clears out the enemy camp and reclaims lost territory from the darklands. This is the re-targeting power of the Gospel, His light dispelling the darkness and restoring life.

Sons target the enemy!

Unmasking Questions:

What areas in your life are easy targets for the enemy?

How can you secure your defenses against his attacks?

How does a target respond to threats?

Unmasking Prayer:

Father God, we trust in your strong hand, we trust your training of our hands and our hearts. Strengthen our resolve, our faith and our vision. Help us rely on your full armor and every promise we have from You. We are men after your heart, we are men driven by your spirit and we are men that belong to You. We bow to no other King but You our God and our deliverer! Amen!

*"And each man stands with his face in the light. Of his own
drawn sword, ready to do what a hero can."*
- Elizabeth Barrett Browning

*"How God anointed Jesus of Nazareth with the Holy Spirit and
with power. He went about doing good and healing all who were
oppressed by the devil, for God was with him." Acts 10:38*

DAY 13 - HERO

Eric Liddell, his story made famous in the film Chariots of Fire, was not only an Olympic champion but a famous Christian missionary. It is his story as a missionary to China that shows the great courage of this Scottish hero. Japanese aggression in Asia made China a military target and in 1941 the British Government advised all British nationals to leave. Convincing his wife Florence to leave China and take their children to Canada, Liddell stayed behind to minister to his flock. That decision led to his capture and imprisonment by the invasion forces of Japan. Liddell remained in the internment camp until his death two years later (just five months before liberation) he was 43.

After the war, Chinese authorities reported that Liddell had refused an opportunity to leave the camp as part of a secret prisoner exchange between Great Britain and Japan. Choosing sacrificial love over his own needs and comfort, Liddell declined the offer of freedom so a pregnant woman could go home in his place. This brave man died in a prison camp without ever seeing his family again, sacrificing his freedom for another, and he left a hero's legacy for all to follow.

"For we are His workmanship, created in Christ Jesus for good works, which God prepared beforehand that we should walk in them." *Ephesians 2:10*

Heroes invest in goodness; they embrace the call to do what God has prepared for them. This investment, more than just good deeds; is a focused expression of the Father's heart. Goodness is fueled by self-sacrificing love, the love Jesus showed us. The prepared work before us has purpose embedded in it and drives our salvation story. Our story tells a remarkable and powerful tale. It chronicles God's redemptive work in our life, a life redeemed to make a difference.

"I tell you the truth, anyone who believes in me will do the same works I have done, and even greater works, because I am going to be with the Father." John 14:12

Believing in Jesus unites our heart with His and that faith defines the normal walk of a son. Great works are possible because Jesus has promised to work through those who believe in Him. We are His sons, His workmanship and an unstoppable force of good works.

In his book Cure for the Common Life, Max Lucado says this:

"Remember, no one else has your talents. No one. God elevates you from common-hood by matching your unique abilities to custom-made assignments."

If the God of the universe lives inside of you, and He does, how could you do anything less than great things? The Holy Spirit breathes through you, motivates you, stimulates you, activates you... does this sound like mediocrity to you? It is our definition of "great things" that needs adjustment.

"There is no greater love than to lay down one's life for one's friends." John 15:13

The heroic measures of Messiah Jesus won our souls, delivered our hearts and freed our spirits. If you have accepted this Messiah, you are now a man after God's own heart. Such a man impacts his world and makes it better. There is an enemy opposed to this plan; the one bent on your destruction. Sons do not back down or concede to an already defeated foe. Resist the enemy and reject his lies. Remind him of the hero inside with the truth of who God says you are.

"The Spirit Himself testifies with our spirit that we are children of God." Romans 8:16

You are significant, needed and extremely important to the rescue of this world. Your life produces momentum, growth and changes the course of history, yes, history. Do not downplay the Father's influence displayed through your life as you journey with Christ. Your testimony, your story of Christ changing your life is powerful and holy; it is how God speaks through you.

There is power in your words, speak them wisely. Your life has influence, live with integrity and honor. There is authority, strength and fierceness in your prayers, never stop praying them. This is the heroic life of men who follow Christ.

Sons are heroes!

Unmasking Questions:

What does the Bible mean to you when it tells us to "do good"?

What does it mean to not grow weary in doing good?
(Galatians 6:9)

What would you be willing to sacrifice for someone's freedom?

Unmasking Prayer:

Father, thank you for the heroic measures by your son, our Messiah Jesus. I praise You for the sacrificial love poured out for my freedom, my salvation and the rescue of my heart. Create in me a hero spirit, fueled by your love and compassion. Give me boldness to live and love like my hero Jesus. In Jesus name, Amen!

"For we are glad when we are weak and you are strong. Your restoration is what we pray for." 2 Corinthians 13:9

"God is the father who watches and waits for his children, runs out to meet them, embraces them, pleads with them, begs and urges them to come home."
- Henri J.M. Nouwen, Return of the Prodigal Son

DAY 14 - RESTORE

Queen Elizabeth II, the current reigning monarch of the United Kingdom has a curious and traditional title. Her Royal Majesty is known as the "Fountain of Honor", a position that gives her the authority of presenting—on worthy individuals—titles and awards, such as knighthoods. She can appoint 1000 of these "knights" a year usually from recommendations of the Prime Minister (or other Government officials).

On December 13, 2003, something amazing happened; rock star Mick Jagger received a knighthood. It may seem a bizarre choice, since womanizing, drug abuse and anti-establishment views don't look good on the knight resume. But hey, he wrote cool songs, so why not make him a knight!

Bowing to outside political pressure, the Queen reluctantly allowed this unusual candidate into the realm of knighthood. Since she believed him to be unsuitable for this honor, the Queen avoided giving him his knighthood face-to-face. Instead, asking her son the Prince of Wales to present the honor while she scheduled a medical procedure for herself.

Mr. Jagger, delighted at his appointment, deflected the public (and Royal) criticism with some interesting quotes. A fitting, "hey you, get off my cloud" response.

"I'm delighted. I never expected to get a knighthood. You think 'This is great' and then are very surprised, thinking 'Why is this?" Sir Jagger continued: "Whether I deserve one or not is not my place. I'm happy to get one. It's great recognition of what the band's achievements have been."

"I think the thing about honours is that you should never ask for them and you should never expect them, but I think you should accept them if they're given to you."

Those quotes moved me, and although one may doubt the sincerity of his words, Mister Jagger expressed something of great value. He accepted the gift, the recognition, and the identity given to him by a higher authority. As unlikely as Mick Jagger was as a choice for knighthood—even more so is God calling us His sons. Yet, God makes the restoration to sonship possible!

Restoration means to bring back to its former state; to bring back from a state of ruin, decay, disease, to repair; renew; and recover. God's design of restoring a man's heart is so much more intense. We receive back more than what we have lost, to the extent where our present state is greater than our earlier one. God's Word defines son restoration this way.

"See how very much our heavenly Father loves us, for He allows us to be called His children, and we really are!" 1 John 3:1

Scripture sends a deep message of sonship that goes beyond what we think of as adoption. God the Father is restoring sons to His original design. When we are restored to a deep relationship with God, sonship is our new identity. This has been the Father's plan from the start.

"His unchanging plan has always been to adopt us into his own family by bringing us to himself through Jesus Christ. And this gave him great pleasure." Ephesians 1:5

It brings Father God great joy to bring us into His family. His adoption of us reclaims every part of our heart, mind, body and soul.

Adoption restores the Father's favor, and that approval doesn't depend on our success, ability or reputation. In fact, God's acceptance of us drives the fear of rejection from us.

"For you have not received the spirit of bondage again to fear, but you have received the Spirit of adoption by which we cry, Abba, Father!" Romans 8:15

My response should be something like Mick's answer, not questioning the honor but humbly accepting it. I am no longer a slave, but a son, with rights and responsibilities that align my heart with Father God.

Sons are restored!

Unmasking Questions:

How do you respond to the title/honor of sonship?

How does knowing God as Father change/challenge you?

What is God looking for in a son?

Unmasking Prayer:

Father God, I am in need of your restoring power. I am hungry for more of your Fathering in and through me. Help me understand this great honor of being your son; help me see You as my Father. I desire to walk as a son, talk as a son and be like my elder brother Jesus. Grant me understanding, discernment and grace as I walk this out daily in You. In Jesus name, Amen

"Above all else, guard your heart, for everything you do flows from it." Proverbs 4:23

"The worst prison would be a closed heart." - Pope John Paul II

DAY 15 - GUARD

The human heart is a fantastic miracle muscle, pumping 1.5 gallons of blood each minute through our veins. Our heart beats about 100,000 times per day (about 3 billion beats in a lifetime). This powerful muscle keeping us alive also creates enough energy (every day) to drive a truck 20 miles. In a lifetime that is equivalent to driving to the moon and back.

Roughly the size of a large fist, the human heart is so much more than a muscle keeping us alive. There is something sacred, something larger than life and mysterious about this organ beating in the middle of our chest. For when we look into the eyes of someone we love, our hearts can synchronize their beating after just 3 minutes. No touching, no physical contact, just two hearts beating as one because they look into each other's eyes.

Imagine the freedom when our hearts beat in rhythm with the greatest heart in the universe. So the Father encourages us to guard our heart, protect it, fight for it but never build a wall to enclose it. Such a wall becomes a prison or worse, a cage. A caged heart can keep a man safe but not keep him alive.

We need to guard our heart from the cold relentless thief of indifference, from growing hard. Protect it from the emotionless dictator of selfishness. The poison of passivity will drive our hearts behind walls and purge passion from us, leaving a dry husk of failed purpose in its place.

Jesus' heart was a powerful locomotive, plowing through the barriers of broken lives to rescue their hearts. I read the Scriptures and see a heart pumping with passion, with kindness, love, mercy and a focus to complete His mission of redemption.

I want my heart to feel, act and love like His.

The purest way to guard our heart is surrender, we keep it by giving it away it to the Father's care. This surrender helps us understand how valuable our heart is to Him. Yes, life is hard, following Christ is full of difficult choices and temptations to give our heart away to lesser things. We fight through hard times with a tender heart, a heart guarded by the Father.

"And the peace of God which passes all understanding shall keep your hearts and minds through Christ Jesus." Philippians 4:7

The Greek word for "keep" in this verse means to guard as a sentry, to surround and protect. Since the enemy also fights for our heart, God guards us with a garrison of heaven's power, supplying peace despite any hostile challenge we face.

"He is not afraid of bad news; his heart is firm, trusting in the Lord." Psalm 112:7

"My health may fail, and my spirit may grow weak, but God remains the strength of my heart; he is mine forever." Psalm 73:26

Our heart is valuable to Father God; He fought for it and redeemed it. We guard our heart best by asking the Father to fill it with more of Him. Our confidence is not in our own heart, but the heart of the Father in us.

Sons guard their heart!

Unmasking Questions:

Is your heart walled off and caged? What do you need to be free?

Read Psalm 119:11, how does God's Word help guard your heart?

I have hidden your word in my heart that I might not sin against you. Psalm 119:11

What are you looking at that is keeping your heart from syncing with God's?

Unmasking Prayer:

Father God, I surrender my heart to you. Please give me a heart like yours, a heart of love, grace and forgiveness. I want a heart that is focused and in sync with yours. Divert my gaze from anything outside of your kingdom; help me to keep my eyes on you. In Jesus' name, Amen

"It is for freedom that Christ has set us free. Stand firm, then and do not let yourselves be burdened again by a yoke of slavery."
Galatians 5:1

"You were created to be free. If you are a follower of Jesus Christ, you're also called to be free." - Erwin Raphael McManus

DAY 16 - FREE

During one of my family's annual visits to the Bronx zoo in New York City, I learned a deep lesson on freedom from an exhibit called the World of Birds. Here inside the large building were various habitats filled with exotic and endangered birds. The habitats, designed to be an open-air display, with no glass between bird and human left me puzzled. It made me wonder why the birds didn't just fly away. Then I saw the sign that read:

The birds are attracted to light, so despite our open-air habitats, they remain inside.

As we left the building, sparrows flew past my head seeking the crumbs of snacks dropped by visitors to the zoo. Watching them swoop and dive, I sensed Father speaking to my spirit. I pondered seeing a "world" of birds inside a man-made environment compared to the real world of free birds just outside the door. I felt hidden questions rise in my spirit, questions I'm sure were from His heart.

Do you want to be free? Unshackled, unfettered and unashamedly free? Are you content to remain in captivity?

All throughout the day, those questions challenged my heart. I thought I was a "free man", one who understood what freedom was. In a lot of ways I am free but not as free as the Father wants me to be. It's more than studying about freedom and it's even more than understanding freedom.

It's walking in it, completely.

Sometimes we believe a flock of lies. These lies fight to convince us we can't be free from our past, our failures, or whatever holds us captive. We believe we don't deserve the gift of freedom. Perhaps we accept the worst lie of all; doubting God's willingness to free us. His Word supplies the hope needed to remove the false habitat of doubt and speak liberty to us.

"And the Lord is that Spirit; and where the Spirit of the Lord is, there is liberty." 2 Corinthians 3:17

God's desire for His people is a deep work of freedom. No cages, no confinement, no barriers, no man-made imposed limitations. Just free, powerful and alive. Father God is calling you to freedom, to a way of living that is so radically different from the one you exist in today. Yes, this life involves surrender, it requires sacrifice but if you will be honest with yourself today, you will see you have already surrendered to something. You have surrendered to something less than God's best for your life. You have sacrificed dreams, plans and desires because you have refused to believe you could be free.

To live free is to understand how Jesus lived. In all his dealings with humanity, Jesus never let success or opposition have power over him. The trappings of success and opposition share a common hook, both will try to latch on and define who we are. Jesus lived free because he remained true to who He was. Nothing changed his message, his purpose, his character or his identity. He remained true and; he remained free.

"So if the Son sets you free, you will be free indeed." John 8:36

Your first step is to believe freedom is possible. With God ALL things are possible! Stop believing in your doubts or fears; believe in the Father's Word.

Sons walk in freedom!

Unmasking Questions:

If you're free to use our voice, what would that sound like?

If you're free to desire (in a Godly way), what would that feel like?

If you're free from fear, who will you become?

Unmasking Prayer:

Father God, You created us for freedom and called us into liberty. With your perfect love you cast out fear and all the lies we once believed. I am not a slave, I am not a captive, I am not in bondage, all these chains are broken by your power of redemption. I am a set free son of God, walking in freedom as I follow You my King! In Jesus name, Amen!

"I pray because I can't help myself. I pray because I'm helpless. I pray because the need flows out of me all the time- waking and sleeping. It doesn't change God- it changes me." - C.S. Lewis

"And this is the confidence that we have toward him, that if we ask anything according to his will he hears us. (15) And if we know that he hears us in whatever we ask, we know that we have the requests that we have asked of him." 1 John 5:14-15

DAY 17 - PRAY

I have never read a passage of Scripture where the disciples ask Jesus to teach them how to preach, how to be worship leaders or more effective evangelists. What they requested was a lesson in warfare although I doubt they realized that. "Lord, teach us to pray," (Luke 11:1) was asking for a heart revolution that would change the way they prayed forever. I can hear the unvoiced questions of the disciples, questions I have asked the Messiah.

What moves your heart Jesus? Why do you pray so much? Why are your prayers so effective?

They saw something different in the way Jesus prayed and it opened their heart to another level of relationship with the Master. They were committing to the prayer uprising that Jesus was bringing into their world.

Karl Barth once said:

To clasp the hands in prayer is the beginning of an uprising against the disorder of the world.

Jesus knew a love revolution needs prayer to succeed. To change a world so dark, so lost, takes a battle strategy soaked in prayer. The world is in chaos, suffocating under the weight of sin, dying from disease, war, terrorism, and abuse of everything imaginable. Every day our faith is under assault, ridiculed in the media, ignored by those in power and fractured by church division across denominational lines.

To pray like Jesus is to step into this battle and declare war on the enemy of our souls.

"I desire then that in every place the men should pray, lifting holy hands without anger or quarreling." 1Timothy 2:8

We need to be men of prayer; it aligns our will and spirit with His, enabling us to stand firm, and act in a manner that honors the Father. This holy exercise invites us into a covenant relationship with God, revealing His heart for the world. Praying is working with Him to bring healing, hope, justice and freedom in the world He loves.

"Or are you not conscious that your body is a house for the Holy Spirit which is in you, and which has been given to you by God? And you are not the owners of yourselves." 1 Corinthians 6:19

Jesus said, "My father's house shall be called a house of prayer." (Matthew 21:13). As followers of Jesus, we are now that house, the place where God dwells. The theme of my Father's house is prayer, where my heart comes to Father God in worship, petition and supplication. My heart is a house of prayer, and prayer is the business of sons.

Prayer is all about love; it's an invitation to love God so radically that your whole life is changed. More than communication, prayer is a connection and a covenant bond that makes our heart beat like His!

Sons pray!

Unmasking Questions:

What does this Scripture do to your heart when you read it?

In these days he went out to the mountain to pray, and all night he continued in prayer to God. Luke 6:12

How does prayer change you?

How important is prayer to you? Does your prayer life reflect that?

Unmasking Prayer:

Father God, teach me to pray like your son Jesus. Give me a vision into your heart so I pray with your purpose, your will in place of my own. Thank You for the invitation to pray to you as my Father, I am overwhelmed by that love. Help me to be motivated by that love and move as You direct me. In Jesus name, amen!

"Life is either a daring adventure or nothing at all."
- Helen Keller

"For whosoever will save his life shall lose it; but whosoever shall lose his life for my sake and the gospel's, the same shall save it."
Mark 8:35

DAY 18 - NERVE

Jesus had some nerve.

Messiah walked with a firm, resolute boldness that challenged the darkness of the world. In so many passages of Scripture He seems reckless, daring and incredibly calm. Our elder brother tackled life with a steadfast determination to restore it to the Father's vision of what life should be. In the book of Matthew, we read a powerful story of the risks Jesus was willing to face.

"When Jesus came down from the mountainside, large crowds followed him. (2) A man with leprosy came and knelt before him and said, "Lord, if you are willing, you can make me clean." (3) Jesus reached out his hand and touched the man. "I am willing," he said. "Be clean!" Immediately he was cleansed of his leprosy."
Matthew 8:1-3

Just after preaching the sermon of all sermons, Jesus commits social suicide by touching someone with a dangerous and contagious disease. In the Jewish culture, once you touched someone with leprosy, you were tainted, as unclean as the leper was. Leprosy was feared, the disease caused horrifying physical damage and the severe isolation laws applying to leprosy, made its victims outcasts and untouchables.

None of this mattered to the greatest heart that ever walked on this planet. Jesus would show the nerve, the courage and the willingness to put His own skin on the line. Imagine the nerve of God to say, "Be clean!" and then make it happen.

Jesus possessed the nerve to challenge this enemy of disease, of isolation and shame on its own turf. When the fight came to Him, the battle plan was fierce and determined. Jesus dove into a full frontal attack on this man's pain and the darkness it produced in his life.

Yes, Jesus went God-mode on the disease of leprosy but it was through His humanity, His skin, that Jesus touched the man. This is the example of nerve and the power of focused love we need to follow. Everywhere Jesus went, through the teachings, miracles, and parables, everybody heard this message.

Watch my life and you will see the Father working.

The early church had a group of people called the parabolani, a Greek word meaning "to venture" or "to expose one's self," they were gamblers but not with their money. Their primary call was to visit the prisoners and the sick, especially those who were ill with dangerous, infectious diseases. Their mission put them at great risk but they loved God more than protecting their own lives.

"And they have defeated him by the blood of the Lamb and by their testimony. And they did not love their lives so much that they were afraid to die." Revelation 12:11

The world desperately needs men to live as the parabolani, the gamblers, the risk-takers, godly men having the nerve needed to follow the Master wherever He leads. Jesus is calling us to leave familiar, comfortable places and have the boldness and the audacity to love people as passionately as He does. Men with such nerve and passion are willing agents of culture change. They love the untouchable, the unclean, the people nobody else will touch or reach out to.

Just like Jesus.

"Your Lord is Love: love Him and in Him all men, as His children in Christ. Your Lord is a fire: do not let your heart be cold, but burn with faith and love. Your Lord is light: do not walk in darkness of mind, without reasoning or understanding, or without faith." - John of Kronstadt

Sons have nerve!

Unmasking Questions:

What happens to you when you reach out to serve others?

Do you like to take risks and feel your adrenaline rush? Or do you prefer to play it safe? Why?

What if you did nothing or risked nothing? What would change in this world?

Unmasking Prayer:

Father, I ask you to increase my love for You and my desire to share that love with the world I walk in daily. Increase my nerve to reach out in love to those who seem unlovable and too far gone to reach. Here I am, send me! Amen

"Compromise where you can. Where you can't, don't. Even if everyone is telling you that something wrong is something right. Even if the whole world is telling you to move, it is your duty to plant yourself like a tree, look them in the eye, and say 'No, YOU move'." - Sharon Carter: Captain America-Civil War

"So then, dear brothers and sisters, be firm. Do not be moved! Always be outstanding in the work of the Lord, knowing that your labor is not in vain in the Lord." 1 Corinthians 15:58

DAY 19 - STAND

Would you risk your life defending a field full of beans? My wife makes an amazing lentil soup but I'm sure I wouldn't start a turf war over the prospect of not having enough beans for the pot. Yet the Bible has this incredible story about a man who understood the value of standing his ground against an enemy attempting to do more than steal a few lentils.

"Next to him was Shammah son of Agee the Hararite. When the Philistines banded together at a place where there was a field full of lentils, Israel's troops fled from them. (12) But Shammah took his stand in the middle of the field. He defended it and struck the Philistines down, and the Lord brought about a great victory." 2 Samuel 23:11-12

The Philistines were a cruel, idol worshiping people, who were in continuous conflict with the nation of Israel. In this story we see the army of the Philistines attempting to ruin the Israelites, either by destroying or stealing their crops. Before the battle begins, even thought it meant their families might starve, Israel's army runs away, leaving only one man left to defend the crops.

Shammah was one of David's mighty men; the king trusted the fight inside this man. With ferocious devotion, against every charge of the enemy, Shammah stands his ground. God produces a victory through a man standing alone in the middle of a field, not backing down from an enemy bent on destruction.

"Put on all of God's armor so that you will be able to stand firm against all strategies of the devil." Ephesians 6:11

The words "stand firm" imply a military stance, for holding a position that is under attack. It implies courage and steadfastness to hold that ground because of a fierce loyalty to the one who asks you to hold that ground, in our case, our King Jesus. We hold that ground despite the fear and the circumstances of that battle. This is the holding pattern of faith; standing firm, armed and dangerous.

"Therefore, take up the full armor of God, so that you will be able to resist in the evil day, and having done everything, to stand firm." Ephesians 6:13

God's mighty men take the initiative to put on the armor so we can stand against the strategies of the enemy. As sons our focus is not on the armor, but on standing firm! The armor is simply the means that we are to use in the battle against the adversary. There are fields worth defending, lives worth defending, and Father God is asking His sons to stand firm for all of them.

"You will not need to fight in this battle. Stand firm, hold your position, and see the salvation of the Lord on your behalf, O Judah and Jerusalem.' Do not be afraid and do not be dismayed. Tomorrow go out against them, and the Lord will be with you." 2 Chronicles 20:17

Sons stand firm!

Unmasking Questions:

What fields do you see worth defending?

Would you stand up for what is right even if you stood alone?

How do you stand firm?

Unmasking Prayer:

Father, move me in such a way that I become courageous to fight and to care in ways I didn't think possible of me. Awaken the spiritual warrior in me to do battle as you see fit, for your glory and for the freedom of many. Help me to stand firm in your strength and not be moved. In Jesus name we pray, Amen!

"Your worst days are never so bad that you are beyond the reach of His grace. And your best days are never so good that you are beyond the need of God's grace. Every day should be a day of relating to God on the basis of His grace alone." - Jerry Bridges

"Through whom also we have access by faith into this grace in which we stand, and rejoice in hope of the glory of God." Romans 5:2

DAY 20 - GRACE

I love being completely surprised by grace. Grace is fluid, an untamed dance of mercy, a song of favor, all leading to God's wonderful gift of redemption.

Ephesians 1:7-8 (Greek meaning in parentheses)

"In Him we have redemption through His blood, the forgiveness of our trespasses, according to the riches of His grace. That He lavished (exceed, overflow, over and above) on us with all wisdom (insight, skill) and understanding (understanding that leads to right action)."

Grace means "unmerited favor, loving kindness" and in this verse, God is sharing His wealth with us. The phrase according to the riches is a powerful statement of His generosity; for God gives out of His abundance! I'm glad it's not according to my riches; I couldn't pay the price for my redemption, I needed heaven's currency of grace.

The Greek word for riches means the fullness of wealth and the word translated according denotes intensity, a force of distribution. In

God's economy, He holds nothing back; there is power and purpose behind His giving.

This Scripture reminds me that there no limit to God's ability (or desire) to supply grace. He gives according to His riches (and He's wealthy beyond measure) not just out of them. He not only has vast resources of grace, our Father is generous with them.

"Let us therefore come boldly unto the throne of grace; that we may obtain mercy, and find grace to help in time of need." *Hebrews 4:16*

The greatest need of every human heart, whether they recognize it or not, is forgiveness. In God's great wisdom and understanding of that need, He generously offers grace. In God's great wisdom and understanding of our need, He generously applies grace to our need. Forgiveness is a deep and full expression of that grace, breathing life and hope into the human heart and soul. That forgiveness begins the road to restoration and gives us the opportunity to travel together with God on it.

Grace is not only undeserved favor, but also undeserved freedom! A rescue mission not based on my performance, attitude, victories, or my failures… just my need. One of the Greek words used in the New Testament for the word redemption describes the price paid for a prisoner of war, the price is paid and they are set free. In reality, we are all former spiritual POWs, ransomed by a loving God and set free to become His sons.

"Nothing whatever pertaining to godliness and real holiness can be accomplished without grace." - Augustine

Sons travel in grace!

Unmasking Questions:

What is the first image that comes to mind when you hear the word grace?

What amazes you most about grace?

How would your life be different without God's grace?

Unmasking Prayer:

Father, I thank you for grace, I know it's a gift, something I did not or could not earn. I love the way it frees me to be more yours. I love how it changes me and invites me into your presence. Revive your Spirit of grace within me; release its power of life in me. Help me to walk in your grace and give it freely towards others. Amen!

"It takes two men to make one brother." - Israel Zangwill

"Though one may be overpowered, two can defend themselves. A cord of three strands is not quickly broken." Ecclesiastes 4:12

DAY 21 - UNIT

Watching the Band of Brothers series moves me every time, I get carried away by the stories of those brave men of Easy Company. I watch in admiration at their dedication to the cause even though they hated the war. My heart aches with them as they recalled the friends (the real heroes, as they described them) they watched die along the way into Germany. I celebrate with them as they see their brothers at annual reunions and for that moment they are young again. These are good men, I wish I knew them.

I do know the men in my unit, here's what I've seen.

One stood with his wife as she went through a dark depression, she's a joyful woman today because of his faithfulness.

One has traveled to the Philippines for years ministering to the poorest of the poor. Many are in the Kingdom because of his sacrifice.

One believed in a friend when no one else would. That devotion helped restore a man's confidence and faith in God. I was that man.

We have shared money, talents, prayers and even homes. It is in these shared life experiences that I am reminded of the men of Easy Company and the feelings they described for one another. They mentioned words like unity, honor and focus, all the while demonstrating brotherly love in extreme conditions. They understood the battle, what had to be done, and they fought the battle together.

I do not compare the stuff my band of brothers has gone through with the sacrifices that members of Easy Company made but we have locked arms through some difficult times and remained friends. There have been times we have stood alone together.

We have sat with each other in hospital rooms and ER's, consoled each other when dreams died, encouraged each other when hopes were fading and challenged each other when we needed a kick in the pants. We have been together at celebrations and funerals, parties and prayer meetings, vacations and retreats and the bond of Christ has kept us. I believe in them and I trust they have my back, in deed and in prayer.

"A friend loves at all times, and a brother is born for adversity."
Proverbs 17:17

These experiences have reinforced my confidence in my unit. These friendships can be described as a God knot, a cord that combines the best qualities of men together. The life I share with my brothers is a testimony to the Father's commitment to His sons. I am stronger because of my friendships; they keep me on a path that makes me a better man.

In my unit there have been disagreements, sometimes strong ones. Unity doesn't mean there won't be disagreements, unity means there can be togetherness in spite of differences. It's dealing with tough stuff, praying and working together for a common cause; it is simply a joint discipleship operation. Brotherly love is the glue of the unit, the strength to stay focused on defeating the enemy together.

Sons stick together!

Unmasking Questions:

Do you prefer to have many friends or just a few that you are close to?

What is the biggest thing you have done to help a friend?

Are you a good friend? Why or why not?

Unmasking Prayer:

Father, You have blessed us with the gift of friendship, a bond meant to unite us under your banner of sonship. Give me the boldness, the strength and the grace to look beyond personal preferences and share this wonderful gift with others. Guide me to brothers needing brothers and help me be the friend that brings honor to you. In Jesus name, Amen!

"Don't hide your scars. Wear them as proof that God heals."
- Jarrid Wilson

"From now on let no one cause me trouble, for I bear on my body the marks of Jesus." Galatians 6:17

DAY 22 - SCARS

A scar is a new patch of skin that grows over a wound. It forms when your body heals after a cut, scrape, or burn. I still brag about one received from trying a jump, on my bike, off a Jerry-rigged ramp in my friend's backyard when I was 13. I wear it like a badge of honor, a tribute to youth's, (somewhat stupid), adventurous spirit.

Scars are showoffs.

I have others, those for years I tried to cover up and keep from being seen. I didn't boast about them or expose them to anybody. Yet, they showed themselves, through attitudes, in conversations and in the way I saw myself. Scar tissue of the soul is not easy on the eyes.

The scar treatment I needed was forgiveness. Redemption had a curious effect on the history of abuse I suffered at my father's hand. It covered the emotional wound and healed it completely, but it left a scar, a beautiful scar. The new patch of "skin" that grew shows His heart and shows off His great restorative power. I am a new creation, one that knows the wound but not the pain it once caused.

"Therefore, if anyone is in Christ, he is a new creation. The old has passed away; behold, the new has come." 2 Corinthians 5:17

That's something I'm proud to show off, for my scars serve a purpose in my life. These blemishes tell a story that what the enemy meant for evil, God used for my good. My scars mark me but I don't let them define me as a victim or survivor. I know I am a new creation, one that walks in freedom despite the scars he carries. My scars don't remind me of past hurt, they remind me of His healing power in and through me.

"Then he said to Thomas, "Put your finger here, and see my hands; and put out your hand, and place it in my side. Do not disbelieve, but believe." John 20:27

What an invitation!

Jesus had no issue with His scars; he invited touch, examination and inspection, all of which gave opportunity for Thomas to believe. He didn't hide them, cover them or pretend they didn't exist. They were battle scars, reminders of His victory over death and the devastating effects of sin. Hiding them would serve no purpose, but revealing them brought freedom to a doubting heart. Jesus wanted people to see his wounds so that they could understand the hope they represented. I want that same heart; no shame or hesitation, no cover up, I want my scars to point to hope in Jesus. Instead of hiding my scars, I want my life to proclaim, "Look and see where God has freed me."

Sons never hide their scars!

Unmasking Questions:

Do you have scars (physical, emotional) that you are ashamed of?

Is there a scar that you are proud to show off?

What do you think Jesus' scars reveal about Him?

Unmasking Prayer:

Father, we come to you wounded and needing your healing power throughout our whole being. We ask that you will empower us to be bold in showing your life through our scars. We pray that our story of freedom will draw people to you. Remove the shame, the pain and the regret we feel from those scars and give us vision to see redemption in them all. In this we pray, Amen!

"If unwilling to rise in the morning, say to thyself, 'I awake to do the work of a man.'" – Marcus Aurelius

"Be watchful, stand firm in the faith, act like men, be strong. Let all that you do be done in love." 1 Corinthians 16:13-14

DAY 23 - MANLY

I consider myself a "generalist" a "jack of all trades" guy. I don't hunt, my home repair skills are suspect and if I judge myself against a list of typical "manly things" I may not qualify for a man-card anymore. At least that's what my dad, and my older brothers thought about my manly skill-set. For years, I suffered from that failure to live up to their version of manhood.

Thankfully, Father God changed all that. He alone defines my masculinity. I don't feel castrated because I can't fix something or track down a wild animal in the deep woods. No, I am a man because the Father says so, because I am His son.

My older brother, an ex-Marine, is one of the toughest men I know. He can build anything, can hunt down (and has) anything, knows every construction tool and its use, but has two failed marriages and left a minefield of busted relationships along the way.

A true man operates out of love, not destruction.

God's men are not defined by what they can and cannot do. A job description is too shallow and easy for our heart to maintain.

Our true identity is not what we project, not what we show off, or pretend to be. Our manhood, our masculinity is based on who God says we are.

"See what kind of love the Father has given to us, that we should be called children of God; and so we are. The reason why the world does not know us is that it did not know him." 1 John 3:1

I am reminded about something my wife wrote about a few years ago. I was clearing out some old paperwork and came across a letter that she wrote to honor me on one of my birthdays. I won't bore you with the whole letter but there was this one section that chokes me up every time I read it.

"Some men build massive skyscrapers, awesome bridges, complex computers, things which can be destroyed. My man builds lives."

It's not our knowledge about tools, hunting or survival skills that cements our manhood. Our ability to make money or seduce women is not manly. The commitment to the heart and mission of Jesus Christ truly defines our masculinity; it's what we love, who we love and the power of that love. Our definition of strength and masculinity has everything to do with God and what He thinks is manly.

"Learn to do right; seek justice. Defend the oppressed. Take up the cause of the fatherless; plead the case of the widow." Isaiah 1:17

Manly skills do not make a man, following heroic examples does not make a man, imitation boldness is often short lived. Real manliness is matching our strengths against the struggles of others and committing that strength towards their struggle. God's man is unyielding and faithful in carrying out the Father's mission.

Sons build lives!

Unmasking Questions:

How do you measure manliness?

Has anything in your past made you feel less than a man?

Who is the "manliest" man you know? Why do you think so?

Unmasking Prayer:

Heavenly Father, help us be men not ashamed of expressing their manhood through serving You. I thank You for men who know their identity is entrenched in who You say they are. I ask You to call your sons, stir up the champions willing to fight for the defenseless, rescue the lost and stand their ground for the Gospel. Thank You for brothers unwilling to be tamed, refusing to be domesticated and be isolated from your heart. I praise You for surrendered hearts and spirits, willing to accept discipline, embrace training and answer the call of the King.

Free our masculinity to be pure examples of sonship, a brotherhood of men ready to be shaped and molded together.

In the mighty name of Jesus I pray, amen!

"Fear may fill or world, but it does not have to fill our hearts"
- Max Lucado

"Don't let your hearts be troubled, trust in God, and trust also in me." John 14:1

DAY 24 - FEAR

There is an enemy of our souls seeking to dominate our hearts, and one of his main weapons is fear. The dictionary describes fear this way.

An unpleasant emotion caused by the belief that someone or something is dangerous, likely to cause pain, or a threat.

According to this definition, it takes a certain amount of faith (belief) to accept fear as truth. This requires a belief system, fear needs for us to accept it for it to have power over us. Everybody, if they're honest with themselves, feels afraid sometimes. Feeling afraid is not the issue, being controlled by that fear is.

We fear for our safety, our security, our position, our health, our family, our processions. This fear affects our choices and the decisions we make. We get afraid to stick our neck out, to take a risk and believe God has our best interest in mind.

Men rarely like to admit fear, especially those areas in all our hearts we're uncomfortable with being exposed and uncovered.

Maybe you think if someone discovers this hidden thing about you, they'll reject you, walk away and distance themselves. And I'm not even talking about a hidden sin (although it could be) I'm talking about that part of our identity we imagine flawed, broken and ugly, undeserving of love and acceptance. We think something is wrong with us and that fear imprisons us.

Why do we give more strength to our fears than the truth? I believe we're afraid because of a fundamental misunderstanding of His goodness. Many times my fear is based on the wrong assumption that God is not good because I have messed up too many times for Him to care.

"And we know that God causes all things to work together for good to those who love God, to those who are called according to His purpose." Romans 8:28

This Scripture boldly reminds us that whatever comes into our life is a part of God's purpose to bring about our good and His glory. Hardship, trials, pain, God uses all these things to work character into us and to free us. God uses these sacred moments, these challenges, to shape our character and drive fear out. We might still feel afraid, but we can believe that God is good and with us through trials. We may feel out of control, but we can trust the Father who is always with us.

"The Lord is with me; I will not be afraid. What can man do to me? The Lord is with me; he is my helper." Psalm 118:6-7

"So do not fear, for I am with you; do not be dismayed, for I am your God. I will strengthen you and help you; I will uphold you with my righteous right hand." Isaiah 41:10

God Himself picks us up and holds us in an upright position. His strength, His help sets us free and when we are free from fear, we are free to live.

"For God has not given us the spirit of fear, but of power and of love and of a sound mind." Timothy 1:7

If Christ fills our spirit with power, with love and our mind with truth, it leaves no room for fear.

Sons are free from fear!

Unmasking Questions:

What would you do if you were not afraid?

Are you afraid of "falling" in something Father God has asked you to do?

Why do we give more strength to our fears than the truth?

Unmasking Prayer:

Father God, You are my God, my help and strength! Walk through the walls of my heart where fear lives and put me at rest. Help me gain perspective in the middle of transition and difficult circumstances. I need your power to focus on your truths and walk in them. I trust in the promise, the direction and the new life you have for me. In Jesus name, Amen.

"Faith is not a storm cellar to which men and women can flee for refuge from the storms of life. It is, instead, an inner force that gives them the strength to face those storms and their consequences with serenity of spirit." - Sam J. Ervin, Jr.

"For everyone who has been born of God overcomes the world. And this is the victory that has overcome the world—our faith."
1 John 5:4

DAY 25 - FAITH

In the movie the Hobbit, Gandalf tells Bilbo that he is looking for someone to share in an adventure. Bilbo, who is taken by surprise by this, answers him by saying...

"An adventure? Now, I don't imagine anyone west of Bree would have much interest in adventures. Nasty, disturbing, uncomfortable things. Make you late for dinner, hm, mm"

After finding out that this adventure is quite a dangerous affair, Bilbo is even more reluctant to volunteer. Gandalf tells him (as an incentive) that if he goes, he will have a tale or two to tell to everyone. To which Bilbo asks for a promise from Gandalf, of safe return from this adventure. Gandalf says no, he can make no such promise, but if he does return, he will come back a much different Hobbit.

This tense moment of decision for Bilbo seems familiar to me, the hesitation, the wondering and the fear of the unknown. Bilbo's faith seems small at the moment, making me wonder about my own faith and then questions like this come to mind.

Why does faith seem like a one way ticket into the unknown?

Why does life seem to require a leap of faith at times?

The African impala can jump to a height of over 10 feet and cover a distance of greater than 30 feet. Amazing jumping ability and yet this powerful animal can be easily contained. If you put an impala in a fenced in enclosure (as little as 3 feet) that it can't see over, it will not try to escape. That's because the impala won't jump if it cannot see where its feet are going to land. It means that Impalas stay caged because they refuse to go where they can't see!

Fear of the unknown keeps them caged.

Too often a personal leap of faith is avoided because of fear because we think we can't see where our feet will land. This is where our fear and faith collide and when our fears fight to dictate our response to a call of faith. The truth helps us deal with that collision, we can trust where our feet will land because our faith is not a leap into the unknown.

Psalm 119:105 helps us stick that landing.

"Your word is a lamp to my feet and a light to my path."

The Hebrew word for light in this verse means "daylight" the brightest light! There is no struggling to see here, His word provides the light needed to see where we're going and where we're landing. Biblical faith is based on the best evidence available, His Word, His track record and everything the Father is.

Faith is not based on what God might do; it's based on who He is! A leap of faith is not a blind jump into the unknown because in reality we jump out of darkness into the light! His Word provides the way, the direction and the path. In the collision between faith and fear, faith steps out and lands on the promises of God the Father.

Sons step out in faith!

Unmasking Questions:

How should we respond to the challenges God sends us?

Why is it hard to have faith in God?

What areas of your life is God asking you to step out in faith?

Unmasking Prayer:

Father, there are times when I am afraid to step out and trust your calling. Empower me with your Word, increase my faith and shed the light I need to see my way. I proclaim that my trust, my faith is in You and You alone. I will believe and obey your Word and follow where You are leading. In Jesus name, Amen!

*"Speak clearly, if you speak at all; carve every word before
you let it fall."* - *Oliver Wendell Holmes*

*"Let the words of my mouth, and the meditation of my heart, be
acceptable in thy sight, O LORD, my strength, and my redeemer."*
Psalm 19:14

DAY 26 - VOICE

Early in my life I had a huge speech impediment. I'm not sure how it happened (I suspect my worn out 4th grade teacher) but one day I found myself enrolled in a speech therapy class with a few other kids. We met once a week with a teacher-therapist person who had the unfortunate job of getting us all to speak clearly.

I don't remember all the speaking issues represented in our sessions but one kid was a huge stutterer. My issue was different; I slurred my way through the English language. When I got excited or nervous, I would slur all my words into one long word. Many consonants and vowels were injured along the way.

So, every week we would gather in a small room and try our best to repeat the words on the flash cards the speech expert would show us. Between my slurring and the other kid's stuttering I'm sure the other kids never had a chance to try their hand (or their tongue) at this exercise. After weeks of slurring and stuttering flash card madness, the sessions suddenly stopped. I'm guessing we drove that poor woman to leave and join a nunnery, taking (happily) a vow of silence.

For many years I was afraid to raise my voice and to speak in front of people despite the call I felt on my life. I allowed remnants of my speech impediment to dictate my boldness instead of trusting the Father to help form the words correctly as they rolled off my tongue.

When I found my voice the ability to say what was on my heart became easier. Since those days of slurring sloppiness, God has helped me overcome most of my slippery diction. What remains is mostly unnoticeable and something I use to good-naturedly poke fun at myself. I have no problem standing in front of people and speaking and even if I mispronounce a word (or a few dozen) it doesn't keep me from sharing my story.

What made the difference?

Believing that God gave me a voice was the key I needed. Discovering the value in my words, even in the way I delivered them, empowered my belief. I'm not the greatest orator, the most compelling speaker or the best communicator you can listen to but I have a God given voice with a message uniquely mine.

And so do you.

Our voice is so much more than the words coming from our mouth. Our gifts, our abilities, our talents, mix those with feelings, opinions and behaviors and you have a voice. It's the sound our life makes.

"Everything in me will celebrate when you speak what is right."
Proverbs 23:16

The Father is celebrating your voice today. It's too valuable to be stilled by imagined inadequacies, or by the enemy's reminders of what you may lack. There is power in the voice the Father has given you, all you have to do is speak up and trust.

Sons raise their voice!

Unmasking Questions:

Is there anything hindering your voice?

If you knew that you had to give a speech tomorrow, what would you talk about?

What is the message your voice is sharing?

Unmasking Prayer:

Dear Father, help us find our voice by first seeking your heart and letting your voice speak through us. Guide our words, actions, opinions, and meditations so that they honor you and express your love. Grant us boldness to speak when we feel our voice is insufficient to make a difference. Give us words of life to speak about all you have done for us. In Jesus name, Amen!

"The measure of a life, after all, is not its duration, but its donation." - Corrie Ten Boom

"Each of you should give what you have decided in your heart to give, not reluctantly or under compulsion, for God loves a cheerful giver." 2 Corinthians 9:7

DAY 27 - GIVE

Our small chapel was filled, a nice treat for a festive day, with a cozy mix of regulars, family and wide-eyed first timers. Our gathering was a Christmas celebration highlighting a worship dance by the young ladies of our church, their youthful expressions of joy deepening wonder in all our hearts. We followed with the carols of the season. The congregation joining voices together in worship, singing "glory to the newborn King" as if we were transported to a lowly stable, personally watching the story unfold.

One of our elders gave a message of hope about our Wonderful Counselor and the power in that title our Lord carries. The message led us to share Communion together; a pause to remember what Jesus came to give us. After sharing the Lord's Table, we closed our gathering with a chorus of Silent Night.

As the service ended I thought about all the wonderful God moments that took place. It was in the post celebration haze that my wife told me that God was working His wonder on us before the service had begun.

God showed Himself during the excited meet and greet mosh-pit of friendly handshakes and hugs that filled our aisles as people were ushered in the sanctuary. In that crowd we saw that our neighbors decided to come, prodded on by the friendship between my youngest daughter and theirs, who urged them all to come and see "Becky's dance".

Her younger brother came with a different agenda; he came with a wonderful mission to give something away. As my wife greeted him, he held out his small hand and offered a chocolate candy from his treasure of three to her.

"I bought these in case someone felt stressed." He said,
his eyes displaying the conviction of his quest.

"Every man shall give as he is able, according to the blessing of the LORD your God which he has given you." Deuteronomy 16:17

That small gift, which my wife gladly received, was an expression of a heart that came to give. That is the miracle of Christmas, understanding the blessing given and going on the mission to re-gift a message of "good tidings of great joy".

God has made giving possible, He so loved... He gave! The blessing of His life through us gives us all "give away" power. My little neighbor came prepared to give all he had. That's how I want to live my life.

We don't give to earn God's approval, giving is a heart longing to connect with God's plan. Sons come prepared to give, whether time, treasure or talent. In that way giving becomes worship, a sacrifice of praise for a God who has given us life abundantly.

Sons are generous!

Unmasking Questions:

What motive is in your heart about giving?

What does generosity look like to you?

How was Jesus generous to us?

Unmasking Prayer:

Father, all that I am is yours, all that I have is yours. Move on my heart to love and to give like yours. Let my life be an invitation that opens doors for my neighbors to come to a deep and abiding relationship with You. Let your generosity flow through me. In Jesus name, Amen

"I would maintain that thanks are the highest form of thought; and that gratitude is happiness doubled by wonder." - G.K. Chesterton

"I will give thanks to the LORD with my whole heart; I will recount all of your wonderful deeds." Psalm 9:1

DAY 28 - GRATEFUL

I'm amazed at the heart of our Messiah. He surprises me with the generosity, passion, and fierceness of that heart. One of my greatest discoveries about Jesus' heart is His powerful example of gratefulness.

His heart inspires mine to grow.

Cultivating a heart of gratitude requires a deep look at Jesus' heart and what motivated Him to give thanks. In the Gospel of John, chapter 11, we find a powerful example to learn from.

In this chapter Jesus' friend Lazarus has died, setting the stage for our Lord to perform one of the most amazing miracles recorded in Scripture. Jesus was going to raise Lazarus from the dead after he had been dead for 4 days! Before He brings Lazarus back to life, Jesus prays this amazing prayer.

"So they took away the stone. And Jesus lifted up his eyes and said, "Father, I thank you that you have heard (give me an audience and understand) me. (42) I knew that you always (for ever more)

hear me, but I said this on account of the people standing around, that they may believe that you sent me." John 11:41-42

I love what I see here in this prayer, Jesus is thankful for His relationship with the Father. Knowing that He was always one with the Father who always heard His prayer produced gratefulness. God is all about relationships. Our greatest cause to celebrate, our salvation, the forgiveness of our sins happened because Father God wanted a deep, loving relationship with us.

Seeking God first brings out a thankful spirit.

The death of His friend and the unbelief of other family members and mourners brought tears to the eyes of Jesus. Jesus attacked this difficult moment with a deliberate statement of faith in His Father! He would not be swayed by His grief or the unbelief of others, He would give thanks.

True thankfulness is not ignoring the struggles; and the pain and fear that haunt us at times. Gratefulness is supposed to be a way of life for us. To be like Jesus is to live a life of thankfulness.

Give thanks (express gratitude) in (during) all circumstances; for this is the will of God in Christ Jesus for you. 1 Thessalonians 5:18

Notice it doesn't say FOR all circumstances, it says IN, or during them. Through difficult times we reach out, we praise; and we express a heart of gratefulness that confesses our great need of Him. Having a grateful spirit gives us a different perspective; it opens our eyes to see God's heart and His purpose (will) for us. Gratitude gives you true clarity and focus on how God is working in your life.

Sons express gratefulness!

Unmasking Questions:

What am I taking for granted that, if I stop to think about it, I am grateful for?

What insights have I gained that I am grateful for?

Are you thankful for the challenges that you've experienced? Why?

Unmasking Prayer:

Father, my heart is overwhelmed with gratitude and my lips cannot find enough words to express all that I am thankful for. I offer myself, all that I am in humble praise to my great King and Lord... the great shepherd of my soul. My spirit pauses and reflects on the wonderful things you have done for me and how your great deeds enrich my life with goodness. Truly I am blessed, your salvation has opened the door for freedom and I no longer walk in captivity. The freedom I enjoy creates a joy that sustains and strengthens me... what a generous Father you are!

Thank you... I love you! In Jesus name, Amen!

"If you lose hope, somehow you lose the vitality that keeps life moving, you lose that courage to be, that quality that helps you go on in spite of it all. And so today I still have a dream."
- Dr. Martin Luther King

"Wait and hope for and expect the Lord; be brave and of good courage and let your heart be stout and enduring. Yes, wait for and hope for and expect the Lord." Psalm 27: 14

DAY 29 - HOPE

I do believe that hope is oxygen for our souls; it breathes life into the empty part of our souls. To understand hope is to capture a vision of how God sees life.

"May the God of hope fill you with all joy and peace in believing, so that by the power of the Holy Spirit you may abound in hope." Romans 15:13

The world is confused about hope. Do you ever hear people say, "I don't want to get my hopes up" because they're afraid of being disappointed? Hope becomes more like a birthday wish—something that they want to see happen but have no way of knowing if it will happen. So they keep their fingers crossed and "hope" that everything will go the way they want.

One Greek word for disappoint used in the Scriptures means to shame, to disgrace and to dishonor. No wonder people are afraid of being disappointed; the emotional scar can be a deep and painful one.

"And hope does not put us to shame, because God's love has been poured out into our hearts through the Holy Spirit, who has been given to us." Romans 5:5

God's love, poured into our hearts drowns out shame. Hope grows in a grateful heart, hope thrives in a heart that worships the Father and hope abounds in the heart where God lives.

I want to be a man of hope

It is important to believe a God of hope lives inside of me. Does that mean that it always looks like I have my act together? That I never doubt, waver or melt under the weight of circumstances beyond my control? No, it means my life points to a God of hope in the middle of all life, the good, the bad and the ugly.

Abounding with hope means there is more than enough hope to share, to ooze out of my life and saturate those around me. There is a generous God of hope living in us, filling us with the life the world so desperately needs.

We are at war with the enemy of our souls; I feel it and so do you. Hopelessness claws at us, attempting to drag us off into the darkness of despair, worry and fear. This enemy wants us to die. He wants us dead to possibilities, dead to hope and dead to relationship with God.

The enemy attacks because he is afraid, he fears people that are truly alive with hope. People who understand their hope is in God alone, these people battle back with a fierceness that cannot be stopped. That's how powerful hope in God is!

"And now, Lord, what do I wait for and expect? My hope and expectation are in You." Psalm 39:7

Sons are men of hope!

Unmasking Questions:

What makes you feel hopeless?

What gives you hope?

What does a man of hope look like?

Unmasking Prayer:

Father, I want to be a man of hope, a man who puts his trust only in You. I expect you to move in my life, my heart and have your way in me. I surrender fear, doubt and shame to your healing power and ask for your strength to help me move like a free man. I want to abound in hope and share it in every area of my life. In Jesus name, Amen!

"Worship is the act of the abandoned heart adoring its God."
- John Eldredge

"Whom have I in heaven but you? And there is nothing on earth that I desire besides you. My flesh and my heart may fail, but God is the strength of my heart and my portion forever."
Psalm 73:25-26

DAY 30 - WORSHIP

Worship is more than singing, worship inspires singing, shouts of joy and other emotional expressions, but worship is a deeper relational connection. Worship is a life that is centered on God's heart, what He thinks is good. It's a hunger and thirst for righteousness and following Him.

Sons worship God because of who he is and what He has done for us. He has saved us, forgiven us, rescued us, and adopted us. He didn't leave us as orphans. No, Father God fought for our hearts by sending Jesus to redeem us. He made it possible to have a deep relationship with Him. These are powerful reasons to worship Him.

What I love about the power of worship is that it focuses on God and keeps our eyes off us (even our past), giving us perspective to see clearly. Worship enables us to see life the way God sees it.

Shortly before Christmas of 2015 my wife got the phone call no one wants to get. She was diagnosed with Metastatic Melanoma, usually by the time they find it, it's too late. I left work early to be with her and we took a walk to a local park in our neighborhood. We cried, talked and prayed but as despair started to take hold something miraculous happened, we started to worship. We proclaimed God's goodness and His faithfulness, thanked Him for His generous love and faithfulness and then the fog of despair lifted and we saw Him in the middle of our fight.

The short end of the story for you today is that a golf ball size tumor was removed from my wife's leg and the cancer did not spread. Christine is doing great and following a path of healing that God gave us insight on, something that was possible, I believe, because our first response was worship.

"Worship the Lord your God, and his blessing will be on your food and water. I will take away sickness from among you." Exodus 23:25

Worship involves surrender to His will and purposes... trusting in both. Trust is at the heart of worship, for if we trust the God who is sovereign over us, who has authority over us, we will trust that He has authority over our circumstances as well.

"I beseech you therefore, brothers, by the mercies of God to present your bodies a living sacrifice, holy, pleasing to God, which is your reasonable service." Romans 12:1

Everything about our life is worship, loving Him with all our heart, all our mind, all our soul and strength. That's acceptable, reasonable, and that's worshiping in spirit and in truth. That devotion to Him lifts our eyes off all the things that try to keep us captive, that try to quiet our voice and crush our heart. Worship sets our vision on the Redeemer, the one who sets us free. Worshiping in spirit and truth changes us and leaves us wanting more!

Sons worship God!

Unmasking Questions:

Why do you worship God?

How would you describe worship and its impact in your life?

How may work and our busy lives get in the way of true worship of God?

Unmasking Prayer:

Father God, everything we are we offer up as worship. Heart, soul, mind, career, talents, dreams, plans... it all belongs to You. With our voice and with our lives we worship You. No longer limited, no longer constrained, we are free to worship you with all we are! In Jesus name, Amen!

"Jesus' grace to change you is stronger than pornography's power to destroy you. Jesus' grace is stronger than your own desires to watch sex." - Heath Lambert "Finally Free: Fighting for Purity with the Power of Grace."

"You, my brothers, were called to be free. But do not use your freedom to indulge the sinful nature; rather, serve one another in love." Galatians 5:13

DAY 31 - SILENCE

I had coffee with Sam (not his real name) recently; Sam and I were trying to catch up after a few years of minimum contact with each other. As it often goes with life, our circles ceased to cross or even touch. He went to his church, and I went to mine, and there were no social events that overlapped both of our very separate lives.

I can't say that we were deep friends when we attended the same church together but Sam was a very likeable guy, he invited friendship. We had coffee many times, talked in depth about marriage, family and work, the usual subjects that men drinking multiple cups of java converse about. We connected, and I liked getting to know him, even when he exposed a secret that he thought would scare me off for good. Sam wanted to talk about his addiction, one that didn't go over well in the church groups he tried to connect with.

Sam was addicted to porn.

He was brutally honest about this addiction, desiring help to beat this demon down and be free of it. Instead of scaring me off, it broke my heart that he seemed alone in his battle. Over the course of a few months we met over coffee, we talked, prayed and addressed issues connected to his addiction. We set up accountability checkpoints and attempted to enlist other men to draw alongside him but nothing seemed to click with other men and it frustrated me.

Where were the other brothers?

My family eventually left that church and settled in the church where I now pastor. As I said earlier, Sam, and I drifted and lost contact. Eight years later and once again Sam is sitting across the table from me and his words hurt my heart. Sam tells me.

"Jay, I don't have any friends!"

Sam is in his early 50s and he feels friendless, alone in his battle. This is the great tragedy of many men; their hearts are vacant and isolated. If nature abhors a vacuum, more so a man's heart, it will try to fill it somehow. Sam fills his with porn.

He knows its sin; he knows it's an addiction; he knows he needs help, and he knows he can't do it alone. He loves God, loves his family and feels absolutely horrible about his actions and yet many years later, he still can't connect with men from his church. When he brings up his issue with them, the group grows quiet and unresponsive. No insight, no acknowledgement of similar struggles, nothing. It is the great silencer, isolated even when in a group, and he retreats deeper in the sinkhole of addiction.

Look around your church, there is a "Sam" in your midst and he needs you to drop your guard and fight alongside him. Silence is a killer and destroys the brotherhood of our hearts. Your "Sam" needs a place where his voice doesn't invoke shame but invites standing with him in his battle. Yeah, it just might expose your own wounds, your own issues, that my brother is a good thing. Men like Sam, when freedom comes, they will fight the gates of hell for yours. We all need a brother like that.

"A friend loves at all times, and a brother is born for adversity."
Proverbs 17:17

Back to back, shoulder to shoulder, no man gets left behind. Let's do this!

Sons are not silent!

132

Unmasking Questions:

How can you help a brother caught in addiction to porn?

Are you being honest about your own struggles with other men?

Are you being honest about your own struggles with God?

Unmasking Prayer:

Father, I am in great need of You and the freedom You offer. I want the strength to defeat the struggles I have with sexual sin and help my brothers with theirs. Give me boldness to tackle tough addictions in me and in the lives of my brothers. Give my voice words of encouragement, words of faith to speak into my brothers. I will be silent no more! In Jesus name, Amen!

THE MAN PRAYER

Heavenly Father,

I thank you for my brothers, for men not ashamed of expressing their manhood through serving you. I thank you for men who know their identity is entrenched in who you say they are. I ask you to call your sons, stir up the champions willing to fight for the defenseless, rescue the lost and stand their ground for the Gospel. Thank you for brothers unwilling to be tamed, refusing to be domesticated and be isolated from your heart. I praise you for surrendered hearts and spirits, willing to accept discipline, embrace training and answer the call of the King.

Free our masculinity to be pure examples of sonship, a brotherhood of men ready to be shaped and molded together. We are an army of free men, bending our knee to only one King, loyal to one Kingdom and faithful to all the Master calls us to do.

We are sons, we will not back down, we will not quit and we will not give our hearts to lesser things. Our hearts are yours, our strength is yours, our minds, our spirits and all we are as men, belong to you. Infuse us with humility, empower us with boldness and fill us with your love. Let honor, nobility, and integrity join our hearts together as one. I pray that our lives will be powerful expressions of worship and service to you.

In the mighty name of Jesus I pray, Amen!

SONSHIP PROCLAMATION

I am a set free son of God. My power, strength, abilities, talents, endurance, faith, vision… everything I need, is from the Father. No good thing do I lack, wisdom is free, grace is free, and forgiveness is free. Insight, knowledge, instructions… all are free in His Kingdom. I will give my obedience, my surrender and trust. I will stand up to my fears and defeat them.

I will dominate my circumstances and be victorious over them. With God I am unstoppable. With God I am more than a conqueror. When I fail, I will get up again. I may slip, stumble or fall but I will not quit. I am His son and I belong to Him. I do not have to prove anything to anyone.

My identity is in Christ and I will not surrender it to anyone else.

ABOUT JAY

You can follow him at:

www.jaycookingham.com

www.strategicfathering.com

Twitter: @strategicdad

Facebook: StrategicFathering

Jay's goal through *Strategic Fathering Ministries* is to encourage, equip and inspire men through the lens of Scripture and his own personal journey with Christ. Jay also hosts ManUp Moment, a two minute radio spot heard on the Sound of Life Radio Network and Men Living Up Radio. He has spoken nationally at Iron Sharpens Iron men's events and numerous men's conferences/retreats/events closer to home throughout the Hudson Valley.

He was one of the 2016 MEN Impact Change Award winners, honored by the Men Impact Change Organization for his 25 years of dedication in the service of men through *Strategic Fathering Ministries.*

Jay's writings/stories/devotionals have been featured in eight books, the latest being *"God Makes Lemonade"* and *"A Man After God's Heart: When a Father's Spirit Soars"*, published by Thomas Nelson.

Jay mixes personal stories, God's word and encouragement in a humorous, laid back style but with passion that comes from a heart that knows the Father's love. It's that love that he hopes to convey and connect the audience with.

Jay and his wife Christine have five sons and two daughters and have been happily married for 36 years. He currently serves as pastor at Bridge Builders Community Church ("the greatest small church in the world") in Hyde Park, NY.

BOOK JAY TO SPEAK

One of my core missions in life is to encourage men and help them see the Father as I have come to know Him. This mission is a passion of mine and I love sharing the message of sonship wherever I can, conferences, men's groups, social media and even better, one-on-one over some really great coffee. To be used by the Father this way is powerfully rewarding and equally humbling.

If you would like me to come and minister to your men's group, please go to **www.strategicfathering.com/speaking.html** and fill out the contact form.

Thanks and God Bless!

Jay Cookingham

MEN EVENTS ENDORSEMENTS

Jay has a very special ministry to men. He has been to our church to meet with our men and God used him to strengthen the church. Without a doubt he is a "giver" and not a "taker"! If you have the opportunity to have him in your church, or at a church nearby, please use it to strengthen your men.

Waylen Bray
Pastor - Stamford Baptist Church
Stamford, New York

Pastor Jay (Strategic Fathering Ministries) is a genuine man of God who is passionate to see Jesus thrive in the lives of others. He is a role model for young men and a recognized community leader committed to racial reconciliation, kingdom building and just being a good friend.

Duane Brown
University Enrollment Manager

Jay Cookingham is, above all else, real. I've heard Jay speak both in person and on the radio. Regardless of setting, Jay's words are characterized by a passionate love of God and God's people. In a world where there is often a difference between what one says and what one does, Jay's life harmonizes these two sides of the coin of genuine faith. From a life fashioned by the redemptive love of Jesus Christ, Jay offers his listeners encouragement and hope through a living testimony to the Spirit's transforming power.

Michael Kimball
Author and Life Coach

Brother Jay's testimony and teaching at our last men's retreat set the tone for seeking a deeper relationship with our Heavenly Father. His deep love for Jesus and his Christian Brothers is inspiring and contagious! Thank you Jay for you faithfulness to God's word and his people!

Paul Steier
City Municipal Worker

Jay Cookingham is an excellent communicator and a gifted teacher. He is truly a faithful servant of our living God and his Pastor's heart is evident as he shares his powerful testimony of faith.

Alan Freestone
Discipleship Director
Grace Fellowship - Saratoga

"If there is one word that I could use for Jay, it would be REAL. Jay shares out of the reality of who he is and who Christ is in his life. He pulls no punches and no churchy lingo. Jay lives imperfectly in humility and grace. That's what I love about him!"

Rev. Tom Zahradnik
Lead Pastor, First A.G. Church

www.strategicfathering.com
StrategicFathering
MINISTRIES